CYCLE TIME REDUCTION

Designing and
Streamlining Work
for High Performance

Jerry L. Harbour, Ph. D.

QR **QUALITY RESOURCES®**
A Division of The Kraus Organization Limited
New York, New York

Most Quality Resources books are available at quantity discounts when purchased in bulk. For more information contact:

Special Sales Department
Quality Resources
A Division of The Kraus Organization Limited
902 Broadway
New York, New York 10010
800-247-8519

Printed in the United States of America

00 99 98 97 96   10 9 8 7 6 5 4 3 2 1

Quality Resources
A Division of The Kraus Organization Limited
902 Broadway
New York, New York 10010
212-979-8600
800-247-8519

∞

The paper used in this publication meets the minimum requirements of American National Standard for Information Sciences—Permanence of Paper for Printed Library Materials, ANSI Z39.48-1984.

ISBN 0-527-76311-X

Library of Congress Cataloging-in-Publishing Data
Harbour, Jerry L.
    Cycle time reduction : Designing and streamlining work for high performance / Jerry L. Harbour.
       p.   cm.
    Includes index.
    ISBN 0-527-76311-X (alk. paper)
    1. Production planning. 2. Manufacturing resource planning.
3. Time management.   I. Title.
TS176.H365   1996
    658.5—dc20   95-25816
                                                      CIP

for LD,
my wife, my best friend,
my constant joy.

CONTENTS

PREFACE

It seems as if everyone wants to accomplish the same thing. That is to do *more, better* and *faster,* with *less.* The *more* part refers to increasing productivity, *better* means constantly improving quality, *faster* involves reducing cycle time, and *less* means cutting costs.

To achieve this goal, companies have enacted a number of surprisingly similar initiatives over the past several years. For starters, companies launched total quality management (TQM) programs in the 1980s. They also started downsizing and rightsizing. This leaning process was accomplished through voluntary and sometimes not-so-voluntary layoffs and early retirements. Even now, such layoffs are still an all-too-frequent part of improving business. Many companies have also been in an almost continuous state of reorganization and re-reorganization, trying to attain that optimal structural configuration. Additionally, companies have launched various cost reduction programs. These efforts attempt to eliminate things such as excess travel, surplus office supplies, corporate dinners, and other perceived-as-unnecessary expenses.

Unfortunately, the outcome of all of these initiatives is that today, most of the easy, low-hanging fruit have already been picked. As a result, companies are finding themselves in a perplexing quandary. Committed to continuous improvement at both the micro and macro (e.g., reengineering) levels, they are now searching for that next step in their improvement journey. Companies are asking, "What should we be doing next"? Unfortunately, there are no easy answers or magical panaceas despite what well-intentioned and expensive consultants tell us.

Yet, as companies ponder their next move, there are some promising avenues to choose from. Just as companies focused on improving the quality of their products and services in the 1980s, they must now focus their energies on improving the speed of their respective processes. Working faster is rapidly becoming just as important, and as profitable, as working better and cheaper. Indeed, creating competitive time-based strategies has become a critical element for successful corporate differentiation.

Fortunately, the key to working faster is also similar to working better and cheaper. That key is understanding our work processes and associated work activities. Many companies, despite rhetoric to the contrary, still know very little about what they do and how they do it. Although there is a perception of understanding, the reality, when closely examined, is almost always different. Basic process and work-activity information, such as cost, cycle time, work flow, throughput, capacity, and required resources is either completely missing or only fragmentary, at best. Although many companies have developed various high-level process diagrams, such diagrams are insufficient by themselves. They simply do not provide the detailed information needed by managers to better run their companies. Sooner or later, whether we really want to or not, we must dig into the actual details of our business. Why? Because the devil always seems to be lurking in those details. Especially when it comes to eliminating time-consuming delays and associated hidden costs.

Cycle Time Reduction was written to provide some direction for this next corporate step. The book provides general guidelines on reducing the cycle time of both existing work processes and new ones still on the drawing board. *Cycle Time Reduction* cuts past the rhetoric and management philosophy of *why* we should be doing something, and instead provides some real insights into actually *how* we can do something; insights that include a variety of tools, techniques, and practical tips applicable to reducing the cycle time of almost any process or work activity.

It seems that, for better or worse, some of us have been tasked in our careers with making real bottom-line differences; not only talking about making a difference, but actually being tasked with *making* a difference. Because of such assignments, we're able to celebrate and share our successes, as well as mourn and be embarrassed by our failures. Unfortunately, there have been plenty of both. But if we've learned anything in our efforts, it's that improvement and change can occur. It just seems to always take longer than we expected and is never quite as easy or as successful as we expected.

Cycle Time Reduction is for the doers; for managers and others who are charged with improving performance. The book, however, does not proclaim to be a magical corporate cure for all that ails us. Many factors influence success besides cycle time. Yet it is suggested that decreasing cycle times can offer some highly desired benefits, such as increased productivity, improved quality, decreased costs, greater responsiveness to meeting customer demands, increased corporate flexibility, and even greater profitability. Benefits that can help us become more competitive in an increasingly competitive world.

Hopefully, you'll find *Cycle Time Reduction* informative and easy to read and use. But of even greater importance, I hope the book provides some ideas and techniques that can be successfully applied and implemented in your own work setting. Ideas and techniques that will help you help your company make a real competitive difference.

ACKNOWLEDGMENTS

In the writing of any book, there are always so many people to thank, acknowledge, and pay tribute to. *Cycle Time Reduction* is certainly no exception to this rule.

Before thanking and acknowledging those special people, however, I'd like first to pay tribute to Frank Gilbreth (1868–1924). Gilbreth's basic concepts and techniques relating to cycle time reduction are as relevant today as they were some 100 years ago.

I'd like to acknowledge gratefully my colleagues and work associates for their support and continuing insights. In this regard, I'd especially like to thank Herb Berman, Dr. Skip Drummond, Louie Griego, Bill Henry, Matt Lafleur, Vic McLaurin, Elliot Montes, and Mike Steinman. Additionally, I'd like to acknowledge and thank warmly those who have survived my many training and consulting endeavors, and who have shared freely and graciously with me their real-world experiences, ideas, and insights on reducing cycle time. In addition, I'd like to thank Cindy Tokumitsu and all of the other wonderful people associated with Quality Resources. Their professionalism, creativity, humor, and warmth make them, as always, a joy to work with. Finally I'd like to thank my parents Joe and Ione Harbour, and my children Megan and Chris Harbour, for their continuous encouragement and support. Thank you to all.

1 ——————— THE NEED
—————— FOR SPEED

In some ways, it almost doesn't seem fair. It's as if we've struggled to learn the game and then, just as we were starting to get good at it, just as we figured out the formula for success, just as we started winning, somebody changed the rules. They added something else. A whole new competitive dimension called speed.

In the 1980s, we learned that business success depended largely on providing the most value at the lowest cost. Quality and cost, and especially quality, became the competitive battleground. As companies implemented total quality management programs, they strived to better meet customer needs. And along the quality journey of the 1980s, we learned a number of valuable lessons.

We learned, for example, that just meeting customer requirements often isn't enough; that customers aren't as good at telling us the specifics of what they want as we first thought. Nobody said they wanted a minivan, a fax machine, or a cellular phone. But once introduced, customers quickly saw the need for these products and gobbled them up in record quantities. We also learned that there has to be a bottom line to quality improvement; that successful quality programs can't be measured solely by the number of quality teams launched, the number of quality awards captured, or the amount of quality training presented in a given year. The success of our quality initiatives must be reflected in real business performance indicators, like a growing market share, an ever expanding customer base, or an increase in returning customers. These accomplishments ultimately add to bottom-line profitability.

But now that it's the 1990s, the old 1980s success formula is no longer sufficient. Sure, quality and cost are still important. In fact, they're as important today as ever. We haven't subtracted anything, only added something; speed. Today's and tomorrow's successes are increasingly dependent on providing the most value at the lowest cost in the least amount of time. Doing things faster is becoming as important as doing them better and cheaper. Just as quality was the weapon of choice in the 1980s, speed has become one of today's most important elements for achieving competitive superiority. Just look at a phone book from any city in the United States, or any other industrialized country for that matter. What do you see?

Right away, you see numerous ads for all kinds of products and services—everything from abstracters to yoga instruction. Read the ads. What are they advertising? Besides services and products, they're advertising performance parameters like cost, *the lowest prices in town;* quality, *the finest quality anywhere;* and speed. Today, we can get our glasses made in an hour, our pizza delivered within 30 minutes, our packages delivered overnight, our car serviced in 10 minutes, our window coverings made in three days, and our film processed in less than an hour. One printing company even advertises, *"Rush work is our specialty."* In fact, some companies are even incorporating the dimension of speed into their company name by using words like quick, express, and jiffy to imply that, whatever they do, they do it fast.

What does it all mean? In short, it means that speed sells. That companies can successfully and profitably differentiate themselves on the competitive dimension of speed. That time really is money and that cost and quality, although still extremely important, are no longer sufficient by themselves.

No organization then, whether private or government, is immune from the demand to not only work better and cheaper, but faster as well. Whatever an organization's business—manufacturing goods, processing information, treating patients—the need to reduce cycle time is critical in today's, and tomorrow's, competitive arena.

Cycle time is a commonly used measure of speed. It refers to the amount of time required to progress from one defined point in a work process to another. Cycle time can be used to measure almost anything—for example, the time it takes to get a new product to market, response time to meet customer demands, or even the time required to make a critical management decision.

BENEFITS

Compressing cycle time not only increases an organization's competitive position, but offers many other associated benefits as well. Some of these added benefits include:

- Increased productivity—A 50 percent decrease in cycle time can commonly result in a 20-to-70 percent increase in productivity.

- Better utilization of available human and nonhuman resources and assets.

- Increased schedule reliability due to shorter cycle times and greater process control.

- Improved customer service and responsiveness, which is critical to raising customer value and satisfaction.

- Decreased costs, which translates into bottom line savings.

- Decreased crisis management, which allows more work to be treated in a routine manner and not on an emergency or rush basis.

- Increased ability to exploit opportunities, which means organizations can more effectively adapt to rapidly changing market conditions.

George Stalk of the Boston Consulting Group quantifies some of the costs and benefits associated with time-based competitive strategies. He refers to these costs and benefits as the Rules of Response.[1] The Rules of Response consist of the following four rules:

- The 0.5-to-5 rule.
- The 3/3 rule.
- The 1/4-2-20 rule.
- The 3 by 2 rule.

The 0.5-to-5 rule states that most products and services receive value only 0.5 to 5 percent of the time that they are in the value delivery system of their respective companies. This means that 95 to 99.5 percent of the time, products and services are engaged in non-value-adding activities, mostly in the form of delays that add only time and cost to any work process.

The 3/3 rule states that the 95 to 99.5 percent of wasted time experienced by services and products can be divided almost equally among the following three elements:

- The time required to complete a service or a batch of a particular product, as well as the time required to complete the preceding batch.

- The time required for physical and intellectual rework to be completed.

- The time required for management to make and execute the decision to send the service process or batch on to the next step of the value-adding process.

Eliminating unnecessary process delays, improving quality to prevent time-consuming rework, and improving the management decision-making and execution process are vital then to compressing cycle times.

The 1/4-2-20 rule states that for every quartering or 25 percent reduction in the time interval required to provide a service or product, the productivity of labor and working capital can often double (the "2" part). These productivity gains in turn can result in as much as a 20 percent reduction in costs. By focusing on speed, increases in productivity and decreases in cost can be achieved simultaneously.

Finally, Stalk's 3 by 2 rule refers to the competitive advantage that can be achieved when companies cut time consumption in the value delivery system. Such companies can experience growth rates of three times their industry average with two times the profit margin. In some instances, companies competing on the dimension of speed are five times more profitable than their nearest competition.

It is apparent from the work of Stalk as well as others that decreasing cycle time results in many associated benefits, as well. These additional benefits include decreased costs, greater responsiveness to meeting customer demands, increased productivity, faster growth rates, and, perhaps most importantly, improved profitability. Yet, as we learned during the quality revolution of the 1980s, talking about quality and achieving quality are two very different things. So it is with speed. Wanting to become faster and becoming faster are not quite the same thing. However, there seem to be a few basic principles and techniques that, if understood and followed, can greatly reduce the cycle time of any process. What's most impressive about these basic principles and techniques is that they've been known and successfully applied for at least 100 years.

BASIC PRINCIPLES

In the late 1800s, a young man by the name of Frank Gilbreth began an apprenticeship as a bricklayer. During the course of his apprenticeship, Gilbreth worked under several different master bricklayers, each one teaching him a different brick-laying technique. Being naturally curious, Gilbreth began to consider how best to accomplish the task of laying bricks in the most efficient and effective manner possible.

Transforming this curiosity into a kind of lifelong study, Gilbreth started his own construction firm in 1895 at the age of twenty-seven. His newly formed company specialized in "speed building" or building faster and better than anyone else. Under Gilbreth's guidance, his company rapidly became one of the largest construction firms operating on the East Coast.

The company's success at speed building is perhaps best illustrated by the construction of the Lowell Laboratory at the Massachusetts Institute of Technology, which is still being used today. As described by Yost[2], Gilbreth's company completed building the Lowell Laboratory less than three months after signing the initial contract. This feat was accomplished despite the fact that the project was delayed at the outset ten days due to heavy rains. This impressive achievement was described by the *Boston Evening Transcript*, which reported that:

. . . . *thirteen hundred piles had been driven, a million bricks laid, iron beams placed and concrete foundations strong enough to support heavy engines and dynamos, and an adequate heating and ventilating system installed—forty thousand square feet laid out in forty-seven rooms, and a power house besides.*

Perhaps even more impressive than the actual accomplishment was Gilbreth's method for achieving it. Gilbreth would systematically study each construction job in order to identify wasted motion and effort. He would then redesign the work and develop supporting technology, making the job as simple, efficient, and easy as possible. This systematic approach to work design is perhaps best illustrated in the area of brick-laying.

After studying the brick-laying process, Gilbreth was able to reduce the number of motions required to lay a single brick from 18 to 4.5 (the half being shared with laying the next brick). This remarkable reduction was brought about by identifying and then eliminating wasted motions and steps associated with laying each brick, rearranging the placement of the bricks and mortar to a more accessible location, and redesigning the scaffolding to increase speed and reduce worker fatigue. As a result of these changes, Gilbreth's bricklayers could lay some 350 bricks per hour, nearly tripling the previous record of 120 bricks per hour. In fact, Gilbreth's bricklayers averaged some 2,600 bricks per day as opposed to the industry working average of 500 bricks per day.

When one analyzes what Gilbreth did, four important principles emerge. First, he identified and then eliminated all non-value-adding motions and steps, which added only unnecessary delay to the brick-laying process. Second, he rearranged all resources (e.g., bricks, mortar, tools) so that they were immediately accessible. This improvement eliminated delays caused by searching for and retrieving required materials and equipment. Third, he redesigned the technology, in this case the scaffolding, to increase the speed and ease of the work process. Indeed, the "Gilbreth scaffold" as it was called, represented a revolutionary improvement in the existing technology at that time. And finally, by eliminating non-value-adding steps, ensuring that needed resources were immediately available and accessible, and developing technology that supported the work process, he created a continuous work flow. In a continuous work flow, work stops only when value is directly being added. These four basic principles—eliminating non-value-adding process steps and activities, assuring immediate resource availability and accessibility, redesigning technology to facilitate process flow, and creating continuous work flow—are as relevant today as they were in Gilbreth's era.

To illustrate the successful application of these four basic principles, let's take an example of something that we're all familiar with; the changing of a tire on a car. For most of us, this simple task takes anywhere between 10 and 15 minutes. Yet, to successfully compete on the Indy or Formula One race car circuit, the task must be accomplished in less than 15 seconds. How is it done so quickly? First, the value-adding steps in changing a tire are basically the same for either a race car or a standard passenger car:

1. Jack-up car.

2. Remove lug nuts.

3. Remove tire.

4. Replace tire.

5. Replace lug nuts.

6. Lower car.

Pit crews of racing cars, however, have adopted many of the same basic principles that Gilbreth discovered some 100 years earlier. They have eliminated many of the wasted motions and steps in between the six value-adding steps, all needed resources (jack, tires, tools) are immediately accessible to optimize process speed, special technology (e.g., the jack) has been developed to accomplish the task of changing tires in as little time as possible, and pit crews have created continuous flow, so that work flows continuously and is uninterrupted by needless delays. Once again, speed has been achieved by eliminating unnecessary and non-value-adding steps and motions, assuring immediate resource availability, redesigning and implementing new technology, and creating continuous flow.

The racing car example further illustrates one other key element in cycle time reduction not specifically mentioned by Gilbreth—teamwork. In many instances, speed is dependent upon the coordination and integration of people at the work team level as well as at the divisional and organizational level. Management's ability to effectively develop cross-functional work teams focused on completing a specific work activity is essential to the ultimate success of many cycle time reduction initiatives.

Although few of us lay bricks or change tires on race cars for a living, the following basic principles just outlined can be applied to any work setting. Indeed, the following five basic principles seem to represent almost universal guidelines for increasing the speed of any work process:

1. Eliminate time-consuming process waste, represented by unnecessary and non-value-adding process steps and activities.

2. Provide sufficient resources, both human and nonhuman (including information), when and where they are required.

3. Use technology, especially computer-based information technology, to significantly increase process flow.

4. Create continuous flow, stopping a work process only when value is directly being added.

5. Develop cross-functional work teams dedicated to completing a specific work activity.

Whether making widgets, decisions, business transactions, service calls, or just about anything else, following these five basic principles can result in much faster process cycle times. In the following chapters, each of these basic principles will be explored in greater detail and specific techniques on how to apply them will be illustrated.

OVERVIEW

Chapter 2, *Process Waste*, focuses on eliminating all of the time consuming, unnecessary, and non-value-adding steps we normally find in any work process. Frequently, these non-value-adding steps, called process waste, comprise between 95 and 99 percent of a work process. Chapter 2 describes different types of process waste, their causes, and how to systematically identify and eliminate them. A fundamental concept introduced in Chapter 2 and reiterated throughout the book is that speed flows from simplicity, especially simple work processes. Creating simple work processes devoid of time-consuming waste is a critical first step in reducing cycle time.

Chapter 3 is called *Resource Availability*. Think of how many times an important project or work activity is delayed because the right resources are not at the right place at the right time. Providing adequate resources when and where they are needed is crucial to achieving speed. Chapter 3 explores this resource availability issue and illustrates how the lack of readily available and accessible resources can cause time consuming delays. Both human and nonhuman resources, including information, are discussed.

Chapter 4, *Speed and Technology*, explores using technology, especially computer-based information technology, to reduce cycle time. The chapter discusses how technology can be both an ally and a foe in the quest for speed. In many instances, slow computer-based processes simply replace slow paper-based processes, resulting in little bottom-line reduction in cycle time. Poorly designed and slow work processes are still poorly designed and slow work processes, with or without expensive high technology. Using numerous case studies, examples of successful and not so successful technology applications for reducing cycle time are discussed.

Eliminating process waste, providing resources when and where they are needed, and developing and implementing supporting technology are fundamental to creating continuous work flow. Chapter 5, *Continuous Flow*, explores this important speed objective. In continuous flow, products, materials, information, people, goods, and just about everything else, move continuously in a process, stopping only when value is directly being added. In continuous flow, all process steps become interdependent elements of a larger, single process, seamlessly connected. Although the concept of continuous flow originated in the manufacturing sector, it is applicable to any business environment or industry.

Chapter 6, *Cross-Functional Work Teams*, explores the human and organizational elements of cycle time reduction. It describes how most organizations configure themselves around individual functions and disciplines. Most work processes, however, cut across such categorizations. As a result of this cross-cutting relationship, one department frequently has to wait for another department to provide some type of process input, resource, or service. Creating effective functional "handoffs" then is an important variable in reducing cycle time. Unfortunately, such departmental coordination requires extensive and sometimes unwilling cooperation. Chapter 6 describes how cross-functional work teams can sometimes help reduce some of this interdepartmental dependency.

Chapter 7, *Activity-Based Work Design,* examines the initial design of a new process or work activity and incorporates many of the ideas and concepts presented in the previous chapters. Activity-based work design focuses its design efforts at the work activity level. Work activities are then linked together to create a fast, integrated whole. A general design formula, termed the 7W × 1H formula, is presented in Chapter 7, along with supporting tools and techniques. The design formula provides step-by-step guidelines for the initial design of a new process or work activity.

Chapter 8, *Summary,* highlights and summarizes key points made throughout the various chapters. It also offers a checklist of important factors affecting cycle time.

To better illustrate the integration and application of the basic principles and techniques presented, a generic case study is included at the end of each chapter. Each case study will highlight a specific type of industry or business (e.g., manufacturing, service, insurance, transportation). The described events, however, are applicable to almost any industry or business setting. For example, creating continuous flow in a manufacturing setting is surprisingly similar to creating patient flow in a hospital setting. These fictional case studies and companies represent an agglomeration of real events from multiple companies and industries. The presented case studies are not, however, meant to portray unrealistic or unbelievable cycle time reduction success stories. Commonly encountered problems will be highlighted and their negative effects illustrated.

Cycle Time Reduction includes two basic types of chapters; "how to" chapters and "about" chapters. Chapter 2 addresses how to systematically go about reducing the cycle time of an existing process. Chapter 7 focuses on how to design a new process to optimize process speed. Chapters 3 through 6 are the "about" chapters. They are about a number of factors that affect cycle time reduction and offer numerous ideas about reducing cycle time, as well as some very useful tools.

The ideas, concepts, and techniques presented in *Cycle Time Reduction* apply to any work setting. All industries and companies can learn from each other. No matter what an organization's business, to stay competitive it must continuously strive to do more of whatever it does better and faster with fewer resources. Indeed for many businesses, the ability to reduce cycle time has become the determining factor between profit and loss. Economies of speed have replaced economies of scale.

Although your current organization may have survived the quality battles of the 1980s, is it doing as well in successfully differentiating itself in the competitive dimension of speed? Is your company eliminating process waste, providing resources when and where they are needed, creating continuous work flow, and using cross-functional teams and technology effectively? If not, then you may wish to explore the pages ahead. Enjoy.

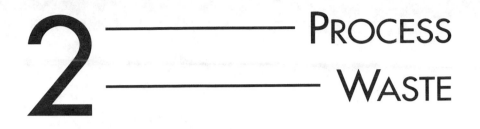

2 PROCESS WASTE

The first basic principle relating to cycle time reduction is eliminating process waste. Process waste represents all unnecessary, non-value-adding process steps or activities. The problem with such non-value-adding steps is that they add only time-consuming delays to any work process. Delays companies can ill afford in a world where speed is becoming such a highly prized competitive advantage.

Although some people equate increasing speed with getting people to work faster, and by association, to work harder, the real key seems in working smarter. Working smarter means focusing on the what (the work process) and not the who. Indeed, when we examine work and the speed of work, the "time devil" is almost always within the work process itself, and not with the worker per se. Therefore, any cycle time reduction effort must begin by first focusing on the identification and elimination of unnecessary process delays; delays that not only lengthen cycle times, but increase costs and lower productivity as well.

WORK PROCESSES

A process is basically the way in which we do work. It can be defined as the blending and transformation of a specific set of inputs into a more valuable set of outputs. A typical work process model is illustrated in Figure 2.1. As shown in the model, inputs are transformed into outputs via some process. Process outputs go to customers, who can be either internal or external to an organization. Typical process outputs include producing a product, providing a service, or completing a task. Frequently, outputs from one process become inputs

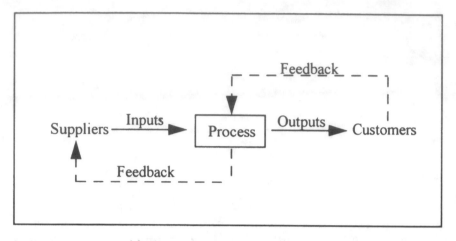

FIGURE 2.1. A simplified process model.

for a subsequent process. In such instances, a dependent relationship between one process and another is created.

Process inputs can include such things as people, materials, supplies, semifinished products, equipment, services from others, or information. Some of these inputs, such as supplies, materials, or services, come from external suppliers. External suppliers represent groups outside or external to a company or organization. Process inputs can also be thought of as *resources*. Resources are required at various stages in a process in order to keep the process moving forward. When resources are not immediately available, delays result. Process speed, therefore, is also dependent on having the right resources at the right place at the right time. This important cycle time and resource relationship is explored in Chapter 3.

Some people divide a large process into subprocesses, subprocesses into activities, activities into tasks, and tasks into individual process steps. However, it is frequently much easier to use a hierarchy of step, activity, and process instead, thereby eliminating subprocesses and tasks altogether. This *step-activity-process* convention will be used in the following chapters. A *step* represents the fundamental unit of any work process, and there are six basic types of process steps: operation, transportation, delay, inspection, storage, and rework. An *activity* represents a natural grouping of associated process steps. Various related work activities comprise a *process*.

All work processes, irrespective of type, should exhibit a number of key performance characteristics or parameters. Processes should be:

- Effective—having the desired quality effect on the receiving customer, whether that customer is internal or external.

- Reliable—consistently having the desired quality effect on the receiving customer.

- Cost efficient—costing as little as possible.

- Safe—providing protection for both workers and the surrounding populace and environment.

- Fast—transforming inputs into effective outputs as rapidly as possible.

As noted earlier, this "fast" concept is commonly captured under the heading of *cycle time*. Cycle time is the amount of time required to progress from one defined point in a process to another. As long as a beginning and end is specified, the concept of cycle time can be applied to any process or related work activity. *Total cycle time* commonly refers to the amount of time required to progress from the beginning to the end of an entire process. Once again, the process must be defined and the beginning and end stages clearly identified.

For example, total cycle time may refer to the amount of time from beginning to end to design, manufacture, and deliver a new product. This total cycle time can also be divided into a series of smaller cycle times, such as the time to manufacture a specific component of the product. Whereas cycle time may represent only a portion of a process, total cycle time represents an entire process from beginning to end.

Critical-path cycle time is often used for processes that contain parallel pathways with differing time segments. For example, when turning around a commercial passenger jet at an airport, a number of parallel activities occur. These include unloading and loading passengers, unloading and loading baggage, servicing the plane, conducting the preflight check, etc. The process pathway that consumes the most time is termed the critical path. The total time associated with only the critical path is termed the critical-path cycle time.

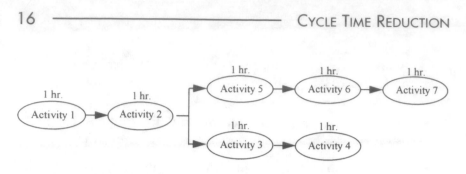

FIGURE 2.2. In this example, critical path is represented by the combined times of Activities 1, 2, 5, 6, and 7.

For example, a process containing seven major activities may split or diverge from linear process flow to parallel flow after activity #2, illustrated graphically in Figure 2.2, along with associated times for each activity. The critical-path cycle time in Figure 2.2 includes the activity times associated with the upper flow path represented by activities 1 + 2 + 5 + 6 + 7. This total time is five hours. Conversely, the time associated with the lower path, represented by activities 1 + 2 + 3 + 4, is only four hours. This is one hour less than the critical-path cycle time of the upper flow path. In this example, reducing cycle times of activities 3 and 4 will not reduce critical-path cycle time.

Theoretical cycle time is another useful time concept. It represents an ideal cycle time goal. One company, for example, thought it had an extremely fast process, bragging that it was almost approaching best in class. Total cycle time averaged about four days. However, when the company calculated theoretical cycle time, measuring only the times associated with value-adding steps, they found that it was just four minutes! What was thought to be an extremely efficient process was actually very inefficient. Theoretical cycle time then is the amount of time consumed by only value-adding steps in a process.

For example, a total cycle time of 100 days containing only 10 percent total value-added steps has a theoretical cycle time of:

$$10\% \times 100 \text{ days} = 10 \text{ days}$$

If the total cycle time is 100 days and the theoretical cycle time is 10 days, we can say the current process is "10 times theoretical cycle time." By employing the concept of theoretical cycle time, companies can set specific goals in their cycle time reduction initiatives. For example, they may wish to first reach seven times theoretical cycle time, then four times theoretical cycle time, then two times theoretical cycle time, and so on.

What's disturbing about most companies, however, is that they have absolutely no idea what any of their cycle times are, real or theoretical. That is, they have never attempted to systematically map and measure any of their work processes. Without such systematically collected quantitative data, most cycle time reduction initiatives become little more than an exercise involving people sitting around a table expressing unsubstantiated personal opinions. Subsequent changes from such sessions usually result in little bottom-line improvement.

When dealing with any work process, it is also important to keep the key process performance variables—effectiveness, reliability, safety, cost, and speed—somewhat in balance. The goal is to usually optimize all or a particular set of these key process performance variables and not to maximize any one variable at the expense of the others.

For example, using a different computer keyboard other than the traditional QWERTY keyboard we're all so used to may significantly increase typing speed. Unfortunately, such gains may only be temporary, at best. The increased typing speed may actually cause debilitating health problems associated with repetitive motion injuries. Therefore, our goal can't be speed above all else. As in the keyboard example, speed must be optimally balanced with the health and safety of the worker as well.

To maintain this process balance, organizations frequently use a family of performance measurements. These measurements usually represent four-to-six key elements of performance. Such elements may include specific measures of productivity, timeliness, customer satisfaction, safety, market share, utilization, and throughput.

In addition, one should never attempt to reduce the cycle time of an ineffective or unreliable process. The only thing that normally results from such efforts is that now the process can turn out bad outputs even faster, creating an even larger group of dissatisfied customers. Attempts to create effective and reliable processes should always precede, or at least parallel, attempts to create faster processes.

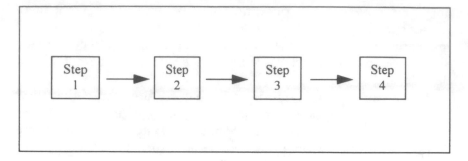

FIGURE 2.3. A traditional "box & arrow" process flow diagram.

Process Steps

When inputs are transformed into outputs, a number of individual process steps are performed. We frequently record such steps in a process flow diagram, as illustrated graphically in Figure 2.3. As shown in Figure 2.3, the process flow is depicted by a series of boxes with action "do steps" in them—do step 1, do step 2, do step 3, and so on. To show some type of linear relationship among the various steps, we also place arrows between the boxes. Unfortunately, this common box and arrow representation hides most of the process waste that adds time consuming delays. Remember, most processes contain 95 to 99.5 percent waste, represented by non-value-adding process steps. The boxes of a typical box-and-arrow process flow diagram normally depict only the tip of the cycle time iceberg—the 0.5 to 5 percent of value-adding steps. It's the arrows that normally contain all of the waste.

To illustrate this hidden process waste, let's look at a typical example. In order to get simple repairs done at Company X, a Repair Request Form must first be filled out and sent to maintenance for approval before the repair work can begin. As illustrated in Figure 2.4, this is supposedly only a two-step process. Step 1 is "fill out form" and Step 2 is "approve form." However, when we examine this simple two-step process a bit closer, it quickly becomes much more complicated. Let's see what really happens during this supposedly simple process and examine it from the form's perspective.

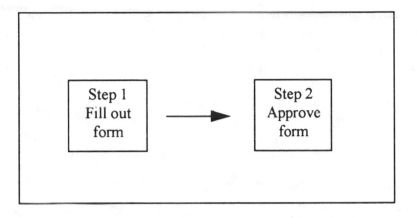

FIGURE 2.4. The representation of what appears to be a very simple, two-step process.

First, the form is filled out by the originator, who is the person requesting the work. Then it is placed in an "out" basket for mailing to the person in maintenance who must approve it. Sometime later, the form is picked up and begins its journey through the company mail system. Once it completes this arduous journey, it is then dumped in the approval person's "in" basket, where it sits idly while awaiting approval. Finally, the approval person in maintenance retrieves the form and approves it. The approval person then places it in another "out" basket. The completed and now approved form is then picked up and mailed to its final destination in maintenance scheduling. So what we thought was a simple two-step process actually includes seven process steps.

Step 1. Form filled out by originator.

Step 2. Form sits in "out" basket.

Step 3. Form mailed to maintenance for approval signature.

Step 4. Form sits in maintenance "in" basket.

Step 5. Form approved by maintenance.

Step 6. Form sits in "out" basket.

Step 7. Form mailed to maintenance scheduling.

Now, let's pretend that a mistake is made or more information is needed. In such instances, the form is sent back to the person who originated it in the first place. The following list illustrates what this minor correction really entails:

Step 1. Form filled out by originator.

Step 2. Form sits in "out" basket.

Step 3. Form mailed to maintenance for approval signature.

Step 4. Form sits in maintenance "in" basket.

Step 5. Form rejected by maintenance and sent back to originator for additional information.

Step 6. Form sits in "out" basket.

Step 7. Form mailed back to originator.

Step 8. Form sits "in" basket.

Step 9. Form corrected by originator.

Step 10. Form sits in "out" basket.

Step 11. Form mailed again to Maintenance for approval.

Step 12. Form sits in Maintenance "in" basket.

Step 13. Form approved.

Step 14. Form sits in "out" basket.

Step 15. Form mailed to maintenance scheduling.

As illustrated, this one additional rework step actually adds eight more steps to the process flow. It's obvious from this short exercise why things can take so long, even little things that seem so simple. One firm, for example, found that it took 21 days to process a particular paper form. However, of that 21 days, only about 40 minutes were spent in actually adding value to the form. The rest of the time, the form was sitting idly in "in" and "out" baskets or traveling through the mail delivery system.

If we are to reduce cycle times by eliminating unnecessary, non-value-adding process steps, it is important that we first learn to identify and correctly map all of the different types of steps comprising a work process or activity; even those supposedly insignificant process steps that we normally never even consider.

As noted earlier in this chapter, there are six basic types of steps that can be found in almost any process. Unfortunately, most of these steps don't directly add value, but instead only delay. The first type of step is called an *operation* step. An operation step is usually a value-adding process step. It directly moves a process forward. Most boxes in traditional box-and-arrow process flow diagrams represent operation steps. They are the "Do" action steps that most people think about and record when describing a process. For example, sticking an arm on a widget in the widget assembly process is an operation step. The step is directly adding value to the process since widgets need arms. Operation steps are commonly steps that people or machines do to something to add value.

Another common type of step in a process is called a *transportation* step. Transportation steps represent any action that moves something, such as objects, people, or information. A person walking to get something, sending something through the mail, transporting cargo by jet, faxing information, trucking finished goods to a waiting customer, or moving a component on an assembly line all represent examples of transportation steps.

As illustrated by the example of a form sitting idly in an "in" or "out" basket, objects spend lots of time simply waiting. So do people for that matter. If this idle time is unscheduled, it is called a *delay* step. Such steps include unscheduled delays of materials, parts, products, or people. Other reasons for unscheduled delays include unavailability of needed resources, management indecisiveness, and the lack of required services from others. Any object or piece of information waiting to have something done to it is another good example of a delay step.

If the delay is scheduled, it is called a *storage* step. Storage steps represent scheduled delays of materials, parts, or products. Supplies sitting in a warehouse is a good example of a storage step. If those supplies are sitting on a dock waiting to be stored in a warehouse, however, we would most likely call it a delay step. Once the supplies are stored inside the warehouse, it becomes a storage step. Supposedly, humans cannot be stored, only delayed. Human waiting time then is always classified as a delay step.

Many types of *inspection* steps can also be found in a work process. Inspections include quality and quantity inspections, reviews, and authorizations. In the previous maintenance repair request form example, the required authorization from the maintenance department is a type of inspection step. The inspection step's purpose is to check and approve the work of another person. A typical factory quality check on a finished product is another good example of an inspection step.

Sometimes mistakes are made and we have to go back and do something over. Such steps are called *rework* steps and represent any unnecessarily repeated operation step. Rework steps are frequently caused by quality defects. They can also be caused by a poor process design that requires an operation, transportation, or other process step to be repeated. For example, collecting information once at the source is an operation step. Having to collect the same data a second time, however, represents a rework step. It is repeating something that has already been previously done. Another common type of rework step associated with information is first recording information in a paper format (an operation step) and then entering that exact same information again into a computer (a rework step).

Process steps can also be combined. Typically, an operation step is combined with an inspection, delay, transportation, or another operation step. This results in a combined operation/inspection, operation/delay, operation/transportation, or operation/operation step.

The six basic process steps are summarized in Table 2.1. Also shown is that each step has its own characteristic symbol—a circle for an operation step, an arrow for a transportation step, a stretched out D for a delay step, a box for an inspection step, an upside-down triangle for a storage step, and a circle with an R in it for a rework step. Combined process steps can be represented by a circle (the operation step) encircling a box (an inspection step), arrow (a transportation step), or stretched out D (a delay step).

Each of these six process steps can be further categorized on the basis of being either value-adding or non-value-adding. One good way to distinguish between value- and non-value-adding is to determine whether the step is actually moving the process forward. For example, in a widget assembly process, a widget body lying on a work bench waiting to have two arms attached is not moving the process forward. This waiting period instead represents a non-value-adding

TABLE 2.1. THE SIX BASIC PROCESS STEPS SUMMARIZED

Step	Symbol	Description
Operation	◯	Any value-adding step. Directly moves a process forward.
Transportation	⇨	Any action that moves something, including objects, people, and information.
Delay	D	Unscheduled delays of materials, parts, products, or people.
Inspection	☐	Includes quality and quantity inspections, reviews, and authorizations.
Storage	▽	Scheduled delay of materials, parts, or products.
Rework	®	Any unnecessarily repeated operation step.

delay step. But placing the arms on the widget body does move the process forward and represents a value-adding operation step. Cycle time then includes both value-adding process steps *and* non-value-adding process steps, as illustrated in the following equation:

**Cycle time = All value-adding steps
+ All non-value-adding steps**

Another good way to differentiate between value-adding and non-value-adding steps is to ask yourself, as a customer or consumer, "Am I willing to pay money for this particular process step?" For example, you're at a nice hotel and want to have a cup of coffee. You go down to the coffee shop and end up standing in line for 10 minutes (a delay step). Are you willing to pay the hotel money for this additional delay step? Did the 10-minute waiting time add value to your coffee? Obviously, the answer is no. Most of us are only willing to pay for the coffee, not for the delay associated with getting the coffee.

A third way to differentiate between value-adding and non-value-adding is to determine if a process step were to be eliminated, would the value of the final output be negatively affected? For example, if we're assembling a widget, not attaching an arm (an operation step) can definitely affect the value of the output. Everyone wants widgets with arms. However, the amount of time the widget spends sitting on a workbench waiting to receive arms (a delay step) or the amount of time it takes the assembler to walk over to a parts bin to get the widget arms (a transportation step), doesn't directly affect the value of the output. If such delay and transportation steps take two minutes or 20 minutes, the value of the final assembled widget is not affected. Neither does the amount of time we spend standing in line affect the quality of the coffee we are buying. Nor does the time we spend searching for information affect the quality of the information we finally retrieve.

As we will learn, in most instances, only operation steps truly add value. The key to cycle time reduction then is to eliminate or minimize all of the other non-value-adding process steps whenever possible. Such steps do not move a process forward or directly add value to the final output, but only add unnecessary delay and associated cost.

PROCESS FLOW MAPPING

By using the various step symbols illustrated in Table 2.1, a process can be mapped at almost any level of detail, from a macro to a micro level. For example, our two-step maintenance repair-form process, which is really a seven-step process if no mistakes are made and a 15-step process if a mistake is made, looks like this for the seven-step, mistake-free version.

$$\bigcirc \mathrel{D} \Rightarrow \mathrel{D} \square \mathrel{D} \Rightarrow$$

And like this for the 15-step with a mistake version.

$$\bigcirc \mathrel{D} \Rightarrow \mathrel{D} \square \mathrel{D} \Rightarrow \mathrel{D} \circledR \mathrel{D} \Rightarrow \mathrel{D} \square \mathrel{D} \Rightarrow$$

Such process flows are always read from left to right. In the above two examples then, the first circle or operation step represents Step 1, "Form filled out by originator." The second step, which is a delay step, represents Step 2, "Form sits in 'out' basket," and so on. Sometimes process flows are oriented vertically and are then read from top to bottom.

By representing and mapping process flows in this manner, some interesting insights can be gained. For example, it is very difficult, if not impossible, to add only one step to a process. When we add a step, we're frequently forced to add others as well, such as additional transportation and delay steps. Sending something out to be reviewed—an inspection step—is especially bad for this reason because it almost always includes associated transportation and delay steps. Yet whenever we experience any type of problem, our first impulse is to add another check or review step to a process. What we don't realize, however, is the negative effect this supposedly simple addition of one step has on cycle time.

Figure 2.5 illustrates what typically happens to a process when we think we're only adding one inspection step after each operation step. As illustrated in Figure 2.5, a four-step process (two operation steps and two transportation steps) quickly becomes a 15-step process due to additional delay and transportation steps that accompany each inspection step. Conversely, eliminating a process step, such as an inspection step, commonly removes three or four other associated steps, as well. That is why eliminating process steps is so important in reducing cycle time. Eliminating one step usually means eliminating three or four other non-value-adding steps at the same time.

In the example in Figure 2.5, we may be able to eliminate 11 of those 15 process steps by simply combining an operation step and an

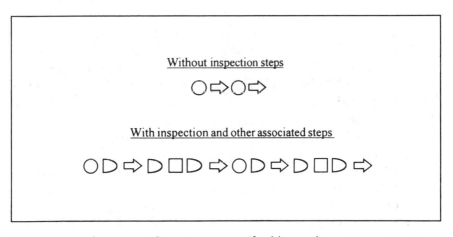

FIGURE 2.5. The potential consequences of adding only two inspection steps to a process.

inspection step into one combined operation/inspection step. Such combined operation and inspection steps are called *source inspections*, since they occur right at the source (i.e., at the operation itself). Our new process design would now look like this:

An added advantage in using source inspections whenever possible is that we're no longer moving a defect through the process stream to be caught, hopefully, by someone later. Instead, if a defect does occur, it is identified and immediately fixed at its operational source and not passed along.

Another observation that can be illustrated from this type of symbolic process flow mapping is just how complex most processes are, even supposedly very simple and insignificant ones. When only a traditional box-and-arrow approach is used, most processes look fairly simple. However, when all process steps are systematically mapped, processes quickly become quite lengthy, even supposedly simple ones. One company, for example, found that simply ordering a piece of commonly used equipment actually entailed over 80 individual process steps and involved some 12 people. Yet, when a group of employees supposedly knowledgeable about the process were asked how many steps the process entailed, most answered, "About a half dozen." They were astonished to see the actual complexity of this supposedly simple process.

One reason then why companies have such complex *big* processes is because they have such complex *little* processes. The complex big processes are an agglomeration of all of the complex little processes. And the reason why little processes are so complex is because of all of the non-value-adding process steps they contain. This is why in cycle time reduction, the time devil is usually found in the details—in the insignificant small things that we normally never think of. Few of us would focus on the number of motions required in laying a single brick. Yet, by doing so, Frank Gilbreth was able to lay five times as many bricks as his nearest competition.

In addition, many small, repetitive processes occur with very high frequencies. Eliminating small amounts of time in such high-frequency processes can represent huge overall savings in cycle time, as well as corresponding increases in productivity. One company found that simply eliminating one half second from a repetitive, high-frequency process could increase overall productivity by 40,000 units per year.

By graphically representing all included process steps, we can illustrate how few value-adding steps are in a given process. Remember Stalk's 0.5 to 5 rule described in Chapter 1? The rule describes how most products and services receive value only 0.5 to 5 percent of the time that they are in the value delivery system of their respective companies. When we graphically map process flows, the value-adding steps, represented mostly by operational circles, become lost in a sea of stretched out Ds, arrows, squares, and upside-down triangles. If there is repeated rework due to poor quality, all of the non-value-adding steps only multiply. Unfortunately, the more stretched out Ds, arrows, squares, and upside-down triangles that occur in a process, the longer the cycle times are.

Such excessive cycle times can be illustrated in the following example. A furniture store located in a small city normally did not carry a large inventory of furniture in stock. Instead, the store routinely ordered goods for its customers directly from the manufacturer. Yet, many customers were dissatisfied with the store's service because it took so long to receive anything—routinely between 4 and 6 weeks. A high-level process flow diagram of the shipping process used by the store is shown in Figure 2.6. The diagram quickly identifies most of the reason for the lengthy waiting period.

As illustrated in Figure 2.6, the needed furniture is initially ordered directly from the manufacturer—so far, so good. But then the manufacturer ships the ordered furniture to a regional warehouse maintained by the furniture chain with which the store is affiliated. There, the furniture is unloaded and temporarily stored. The furniture is later reloaded and shipped on to the store that ordered it in the first place. Arriving at the store, the furniture is once again unloaded and temporarily stored in the store's receiving warehouse. Finally, the furniture is reloaded and delivered to an increasingly impatient customer. One only has to ask what would happen if the goods were shipped directly to the customer from the manufacturer—if all of the unnecessary, repeated, and redundant loading, unloading, and intermediate storage steps were simply eliminated?

Another interesting observation to be made from this type of process mapping is that the cost for each type of process step is usually about the same. The old saying "It all pays the same" is actually

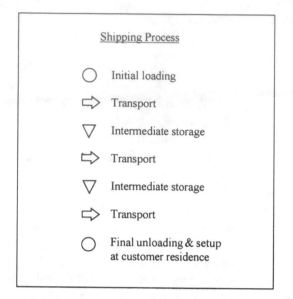

FIGURE 2.6. A high-level process flow of a shipping process. Note intermediate storage steps.

frequently true. One company for example, found that it was paying millions of dollars annually for its service technicians to simply walk back and forth to their vans to look up needed information in bulky service manuals. The manuals were too heavy and awkward to carry directly to the job site. So every time the technicians needed some piece of required information, they were forced to stop working and walk back to their service vans. Once at their vans, they spent additional time searching for the information in the poorly organized manuals.

The company realized that having their service personnel use the information directly added value to the service process. However, the time spent in retrieving the information didn't add value. Yet, both activities were costing the company exactly the same. That is, the company was paying the same amount of money per hour to retrieve information as it was to use the information.

As a solution, the company put the needed information on CD-ROM and gave each of the service personnel a notebook computer with a CD-ROM drive. Now, along with their tool kits, the technicians carry their notebook computers directly to the job site. This re-

design change completely eliminated the repeated walking ba(
forth, transportation steps, as well as greatly reduced delay times associated with searching for needed information.

These examples illustrate the importance of identifying and then
eliminating process waste in any cycle time reduction initiative. In the
next section, a systematic method for going about this process waste
"hunt-and-destroy" mission will be described.

PROCESS ANALYSIS

The elimination of unnecessary and non-value-adding process steps
rarely just happens. Rather, it usually comes about through systematic process analysis and redesign. A process analysis achieves the following:

- Describes the different types of steps associated with a particular process.

- Identifies both value-adding and non-value-adding process
  steps.

- Maps the overall flow of a process or work activity.

- Collects quantitative data, such as time, cost, and required resources.

- Identifies and makes improvements based on factual data.

There are two basic types of process analyses. One type is commonly called a *process task analysis*. The other is called a *process product* or *object analysis*. A process task analysis focuses on a human or
machine activity—what a human or machine is doing to something.
A process product analysis focuses on what is being done to an object. For example, we can examine what a human must do to fill out a
procurement form. That would be a type of process task analysis—we
become one with the human. Another example of a process task
analysis is analyzing what a machine is doing to a part. In this case,
we become one with the machine.

We can also analyze a process from the perspective of what is happening to an object itself as it moves through a process—a process
product or object analysis. In the example of the procurement form,

in a process product analysis we would become one with the form. That is, as a form, we would sit idly in an "in" basket, travel through the mail system, etc. Frequently, most people conduct only a process task analysis, viewing a process only from the perspective of what humans or machines are doing to something. Commonly, however, we can learn much more about a process by becoming one with the object, whether that object is a widget being manufactured, information being processed, goods being shipped, or even a customer being served. In fact, service companies can learn a great deal by conducting a process product analysis with the "object" being the customer.

To give such process analyses a more systematic approach, there is the Seven-Step PI (Process Improvement) Method.[1] The Seven-Step PI Method is an excellent way to reduce cycle times through the systematic identification of time consuming process delays. The seven steps of the PI method include:

1. Define process boundaries.

2. Observe and describe process steps and flow.

3. Collect process-related data.

4. Analyze collected data.

5. Identify improvement areas.

6. Develop improvements.

7. Implement and monitor improvements.

The Seven Step PI Method can be used to examine a work process at almost any level of detail, from a macro overview to a close-up micro view.

Step 1 is define process boundaries. This first step is nothing more than identifying exactly what will be analyzed and ultimately improved. Although it sounds obvious, it's amazing how many process improvement efforts fail to define specifically what process is to be improved. As a result, months are spent getting nowhere.

Once a candidate process or activity is identified for cycle time reduction, it is important also to identify specific beginning and end points. That is, to state exactly where the subject process begins and ends. Additional tasks in Step 1 include:

- Selecting appropriate metrics to measure, such as time, cost, or required resources.

- Determining specifically what to measure.

- Determining the type of process analysis to conduct (i.e., task, product, or both).

- Gaining a general familiarity of the process.

Step 2, observe and describe process steps and flow, is perhaps the most important step of the Seven-Step PI Method, yet, it is frequently the one activity whose worth is most undervalued by companies. Many process improvement efforts, including cycle time reduction initiatives, consist of people simply going off in some corner and flowcharting what they think the process should be, or what they think it actually is. Unfortunately, a work process is almost always different from what it should be or what we think it is. When people describe a process, they almost always leave things out, especially most of the time consuming, non-value-adding steps. That is why it is so important to physically observe or "ground proof" a process whenever possible. It's amazing what you'll learn.

One company, for example, wanted to study the flow of parts through their plant. A meeting was convened and the process flow was mapped out per everyone's general agreement. Then an enterprising individual decided to become one with a part and physically walk the described flow pattern out. The relationship between perception and reality was almost zero. In addition, the individual found that many parts were transported to buildings to be unloaded, unpackaged, and temporarily stored, only to be later repackaged and reloaded with no apparent value-adding reason, except for "We've always done it that way." These unnecessary transportation, intermediate storage, and rework (repackaging) steps not only represented process waste, but inefficient utilization of resources (trucks, forklifts, and people) and building space, as well.

One useful tool to use in describing and mapping process flow is a process analysis worksheet, as illustrated in Figure 2.7. A process analysis worksheet provides a place to describe each process step, show the step symbol and process flow, and record appropriate process-related information, such as time, cost, required resources, etc.

#	Step Description	Flow	Time	Resources	Notes
1					
2					
3					
4					
5					

FIGURE 2.7. A blank process analysis worksheet.

Partially completed process task and process product analysis worksheets are illustrated in Figures 2.8 and 2.9 respectively. Figure 2.8 is a process task analysis worksheet depicting the actions of service personnel. As described in the worksheet, service personnel must make repeated trips back and forth to their service vans to look up needed information. Figure 2.9 represents a process product analysis worksheet. It describes what happens to a procurement form in one company as it is handed off from person to person.

The process analysis worksheet is an excellent tool to use in Step 2. It provides a well-structured method for collecting needed process-

#	Step Description	Flow	Time (Minutes)	Resources	Notes
1	Services equipment	O		1	Normal maintenance
2	Walks to service van	⇨		1	Van parked in lot
3	Searches for information	D		1	In service manual
4	Walks back to job	⇨		1	
5	Services equipment	O		1	
6	Walks to service van	⇨		1	
7	Searches for information	D		1	
8	Walks back to job	⇨		1	
9	Services equipment	O		1	

FIGURE 2.8. A partially completed process task analysis worksheet.

#	Step Description	Flow	Time (Hours)	Resources	Notes
1	Procurement form initiated	O		1	Normal requisition
2	Sits in "out" basket	D			
3	Mailed for approval signature	⇨			In company mail
4	Sits in "in" basket	D			
5	Reviewed & approved	□		1	
6	Sits in "out" basket	D			
7	Mailed to purchasing	⇨			

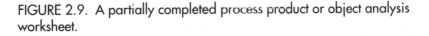

FIGURE 2.9. A partially completed process product or object analysis worksheet.

related information in a systematic manner. Depending on the situation and in conjunction with the process analysis worksheet, a process overhead-view diagram may also prove useful. A process overhead-view diagram is a bird's-eye sketch or map of a process. The orientation is looking down from above and the diagram shows where each step takes place. The numbers on the process overhead-view diagram correspond to the step numbers on the process analysis worksheet. That is why the two techniques should always be used together. As needed, additional information can be recorded on the process overhead-view diagram. An example of a process overhead-view diagram depicting the inefficient movement of materials in a company is illustrated in Figure 2.10.

Another useful tool to use for Step 2 is a process flow diagram. A process flow diagram illustrates the overall process flow or sequence. Each process step type is depicted in its proper sequence and can be assigned a number, which corresponds to the step number on an adjacent process analysis worksheet. A process flow diagram is always read from left to right or top to bottom. A typical linear process flow diagram without corresponding process analysis worksheet step numbers is illustrated in Figure 2.11.

Process flow diagrams are particularly useful for illustrating parallel, divergent, convergent or decision branching process flows. A *parallel* process flow, as illustrated in Figure 2.12, involves two or more parallel flow paths occurring at the same time. For example, making

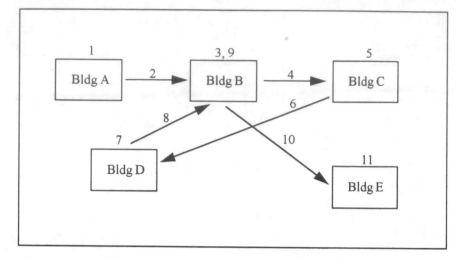

FIGURE 2.10. An example of a process overhead view diagram. Numbers correlate with steps on an accompanying process analysis worksheet.

○◗ ⇨ ◗○◗ ⇨ ◗○□ ⇨ ▽

FIGURE 2.11. An example of linear process flow.

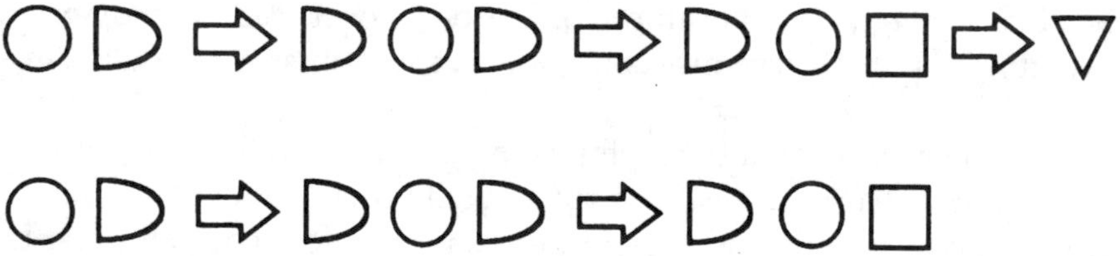

○◗ ⇨ ◗○◗ ⇨ ◗○□ ⇨ ▽

○◗ ⇨ ◗○◗ ⇨ ◗○□

FIGURE 2.12. An example of parallel process flow.

widget arms and making widget legs simultaneously would represent parallel process flow.

Parallel process flows sometimes converge into a single linear flow, as illustrated in Figure 2.13. This merging of parallel flow into a single linear flow is called *convergent* process flow. For example, the making widget legs and making widget arms process flows can converge into the widget assembly process flow.

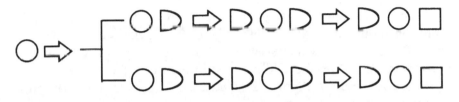

FIGURE 2.13. An example of convergent process flow.

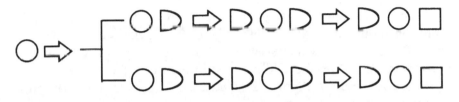

FIGURE 2.14. An example of divergent process flow.

Process flows can also diverge. A *divergent* process flow, as illustrated in Figure 2.14, splits from a linear flow into two or more parallel process flows. Continuing our widget analogy, cutting out rough feedstock can supply both the making widget arms and making widget legs process flows.

Some processes can also contain decision points. Based on the decision made, the process branches along one or more different paths. Such points in a process flow are called *decision branches*. As illustrated in Figure 2.15, the symbol for a decision branch is a diamond.

At the end of Step 2 of the Seven-Step PI Method, all process steps should be observed, identified, recorded, and described. Process flows also should be mapped and appropriately illustrated us-

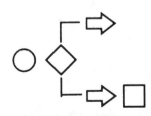

FIGURE 2.15. Process flow containing a diamond-shaped decision path.

ing a process analysis worksheet. Process overhead-view diagrams and process flow diagrams may also be needed.

Step 3 is collect process-related data. Companies frequently make decisions about what to improve based more on fiction than fact. That is, they rarely collect quantitative, process-related data. In Step 3, the goal is to collect quantitative data associated with each process step previously identified. Such process-related quantitative data is commonly called a metric. For cycle time reduction efforts, the most commonly used metric is time.

Depending on the setting, time data may be collected in seconds, minutes, hours, days, weeks, etc. The captured times can be directly recorded on a process analysis worksheet. The two partially completed process analysis worksheets illustrated in Figures 2.8 and 2.9 are now shown completed in Figures 2.16 and 2.17. As illustrated, the time columns, which in these two examples are measured in either minutes or hours, are appropriately filled in. In many instances, Steps 2 and 3 of the Seven-Step PI Method are completed simultaneously. That is, time data is collected in conjunction with observing a process.

Step 4 involves analyzing the collected data. It basically involves summarizing all collected process-related observations. A data summary chart is an effective tool for illustrating the collected data. A data summary chart summarizes the number of times each process

#	Step Description	Flow	Time (Minutes)	Resources	Notes
1	Services equipment	O	40	1	Normal maintenance
2	Walks to service van	⇨	10	1	Van parked in lot
3	Searches for information	D	5	1	In service manual
4	Walks back to job	⇨	10	1	
5	Services equipment	O	35	1	
6	Walks to service van	⇨	10	1	
7	Searches for information	D	5	1	
8	Walks back to job	⇨	10	1	
9	Services equipment	O	20	1	

FIGURE 2.16. A completed process task analysis worksheet.

#	Step Description	Flow	Time (Hours)	Resources	Notes
1	Procurement form initiated	O	0.1	1	Normal requisition
2	Sits in "out" basket	D	1.5		
3	Mailed for approval signature	⇨	48		In company mail
4	Sits in "in" basket	D	1.0		
5	Reviewed & approved	□	0.1	1	
6	Sits in "out" basket	D	.75		
7	Mailed to purchasing	⇨	48		

FIGURE 2.17. A completed process product or object analysis worksheet.

step type occurs in a process analysis worksheet and total times associated with each step type. If labor rates or other costs are known, total costs associated with each step can also be added. On the basis of the data collected in Figure 2.16, a data summary chart is illustrated in Figure 2.18. Total costs in Figure 2.18 are based on a labor rate of $30 per hour.

Data summary charts can be graphically illustrated using a percent cycle time bar graph. The percentage of total cycle time that each step represents is graphically illustrated by the individual bar

Step Type	# of Steps	Minutes	Cost
Operation	3	95	$47.50
Transportation	4	40	$20
Delay	2	10	$5
Inspection			
Storage			
Rework			
Total	9	145	$72.50

FIGURE 2.18. A completed data summary chart.

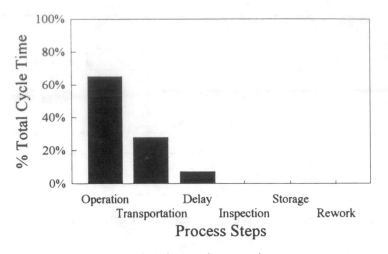

FIGURE 2.19. A percent total cycle time bar graph.

columns. Figure 2.19 depicts a percent cycle time bar graph. Percentiles are based on the data summary chart shown in Fig. 2.18.

One final representation of collected process data can be made using a value-added/non-value-added pie chart. Such charts are constructed by simply totaling up the time associated with all value-adding process steps—typically, but not always operation steps—and comparing this to the total time of all non-value-adding steps. Commonly, such pie charts have the value-adding slice comprising only about 1 to 5 percent of the total chart. A value-added/non-value-added pie chart based on data from Figure 2.18 is illustrated in Figure 2.20.

At the end of Step 4, all collected process data have been summarized. In addition, various graphic representations of the summarized data have been developed.

Step 5 involves identifying and prioritizing potential improvement areas. If Steps 1 through 4 are done correctly, Step 5 is usually obvious. Since the goal of cycle time reduction is eliminating or minimizing time-consuming, non-value-adding process steps, these steps are usually targeted first. Some good candidates to initially target for cycle time reduction include the following:

- Redundant, time consuming, and unnecessary transportation, storage, delay, or inspection steps.

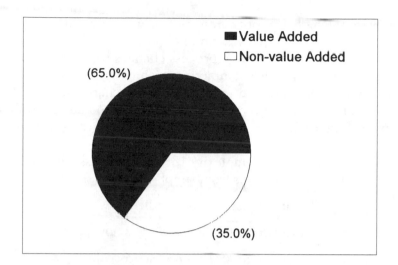

FIGURE 2.20. A value-added/non-value-added pie chart.

- Recurring sequences of delay-transportation-delay steps.
- Major chokepoints that constrict process throughput rates and create significant delays.
- All rework steps.
- Inefficient process layouts, sequences, or flows.
- Inefficient or redundant transportation routings.
- Redundant material handling or packaging and unpackaging.

When looking for areas to improve, it is frequently helpful to ask the following three questions:

1. What is the real purpose or function of this process step?
2. Does this process step directly add value to the process output?
3. Can this process step be eliminated, minimized, or combined with another value-adding step?

At the completion of Step 5, specific candidates for improvement are identified. Also, such identified improvement areas are prioritized, with the higher priority areas normally representing the biggest potential gains in reduced cycle time.

Step 6 involves developing process changes that can actually result in reduced cycle times. Numerous techniques for decreasing cycle times will be presented in the following chapters. The phrase "eliminate, minimize, and combine" is always good advice to follow when reducing cycle time. Some other general suggestions include:

- Reducing process complexity through process simplification. Remember, speed flows from simplicity.

- Changing linear process flow to parallel flow.

- Using decision-based, alternative process flow paths.

- Changing the sequence or layout of a process.

- Using technology as a time reduction means.

- Letting customers do some of the process work.

In selecting an improvement method to reduce cycle time, it is always important to first calculate expected time savings before going to the expense and bother of actually developing the improvement. A before-after chart, illustrated in Figure 2.21, is a good method for documenting expected gains from a proposed process redesign. The

Step Type	Before # of Steps	Before Hours	After # of Steps	After Hours
Operation	2	0.5	1	0.4
Transportation	3	36	1	0.1
Delay	4	4.5		
Inspection	1	0.2		
Storage				
Rework				
Total	10	41.2	2	0.5

FIGURE 2.21. A completed before–after chart.

chart compares the process before and after the proposed cycle time reduction.

It is also critical to calculate not only the time savings associated with any improvement prior to its development, but also all potential cost savings. Such cost savings must, in turn, be compared to the cost of implementing the proposed process design change. As such, an appropriate cost/benefit ratio should be calculated. At the end of Step 6, specific types of improvements should be identified, their time and cost savings calculated, and selected improvements actually developed.

Step 7 of the Seven-Step PI Method involves implementing and monitoring the redesigned process. Process improvements associated with such redesigns are usually implemented as either a pilot run, in which the improvement is tested over a specified time period, a complete switchover, in which the improvement is initiated instantly, or as a gradual phase in, in which the new process design gradually replaces the old one.

The appropriate implementation method depends largely on the complexity and associated risks involved, as well as the associated cost. For example, a costly improvement may be piloted on a much cheaper scale to first prove its economic worth. Also, improvement must be maintained as process gains have a nasty habit of disappearing over time.

Whenever implementing a significant process change, it is important to get those directly affected by the change involved in the improvement process as early as possible. The significance of the human element in such change initiatives should not be underestimated. Involving organizational and team development specialists in any significant change initiative makes good business sense. It may also ultimately determine the difference between success and failure.

An important note on implementation. Improvement can be defined simply as a change for the better. In the Seven-Step PI Method:

Improvement = Analysis × Development × Implementation

With no implementation, there can be no improvement. Successfully completing the first six steps of the Seven-Step PI Method does not equal improvement. It only equals analysis and development of a potential gain. The redesigned process must be implemented for improvement to actually occur. That is, all seven steps must be successfully executed to gain any real benefit. However, one important variation of the Seven-Step PI Method should be mentioned and illustrated.

When mapping a fairly complex or large process, it is not uncommon to identify and map 100 to 150 individual process steps. When this occurs, it is often useful to stop at Step 4 (Analyze collected data) in the Seven-Step PI Method and group the identified process steps into a series of related work activities. Remember, a work activity is a logical grouping of process steps. For example, process steps 1 through 12 may be grouped under Activity A, process steps 13 through 47 under Activity B, process steps 48 through 65 under Activity C, and so on. Usually, about four to ten major activities can be identified in this manner, as illustrated in Figure 2.22.

Once individual process steps have been grouped into activities, it is often useful to summarize collected process data at the activity level, just as it was done at the process step level. Some useful summaries include:

- Develop a data summary chart for each activity that identifies the type, number, and associated cumulative times and costs of process steps within that activity.

- Develop a value added/non-value added pie chart for each activity.

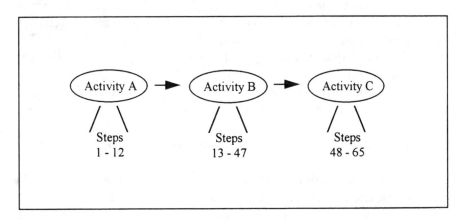

FIGURE 2.22. A grouping of a series of process steps into three distinct activities.

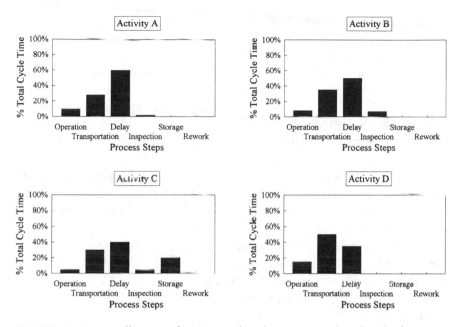

FIGURE 2.23. A collection of activity-related percent total cycle time bar graphs.

- Calculate the percent total cycle time that each activity represents and display that information in a standard bar graph.

Some examples of summarized data at the activity level are illustrated in Figure 2.23.

After summarizing the data at the activity level, one then proceeds to Step 5 of the Seven-Step PI Method. However, instead of focusing on identifying improvements at the process step level, the focus is initially at the activity level. The following questions should be asked:

- What value does each activity add to the final output?

- Can an entire activity be eliminated?

- If an activity cannot be eliminated, can it be combined with another activity?

- Can the sequence or flow of the activities be changed such that process speed increases?

By asking such questions at the activity level, a number of insights can be gained. For example, one company's process analysis resulted in grouping a large number of identified process steps into seven major work activities. After asking the first question—What value does this activity add to the final output?—it was decided that Activity D added no real value to the process and was, therefore, completely eliminated. Further examination indicated that it made little sense to have Activities B and C occur as two separate activities. They could more easily be combined into one activity, with significant time and cost savings. At the end of this initial assessment, only five of the seven activities remained, as illustrated in Figure 2.24. Efforts were then directed at eliminating waste at the process step level within each of the five remaining activities.

The value of this activity-based approach is that entire activities can be eliminated at the outset. This early elimination prevents trying to redesign a process at the step level, only to later eliminate those very same steps at the activity level.

In some instances, it may become apparent during Step 5 (Identify improvement area) that more detailed process mapping is required for selected process step intervals. For example, an identified operation step may actually represent a "mega" step composed of numerous other steps (e.g., transportation, delay, and inspection steps).

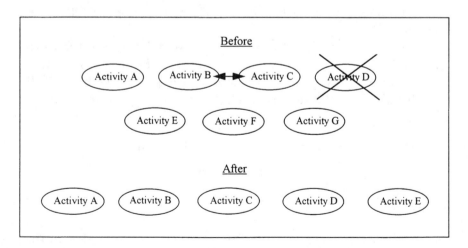

FIGURE 2.24. Just like steps, activities can be eliminated and combined.

It is useful when dealing with large processes to pick an initial process mapping level that allows one to conveniently group steps into activities, as well as add greater detail to a particular step or group of steps later, if necessary. As such, examining a large work process is somewhat analogous to looking through a zoom lens on a camera. Both wide-angle activity level shots, as well as detailed process step close-ups must be taken. In this context, the Seven-Step PI Method becomes an iterative process, and may require going back and forth among the seven steps.

It is perhaps important to note that some people advocate a top-down process mapping approach. That is, process mapping should always begin with some type of high-level process map, which then leads to finer and finer detailed mapping. This is a good and logical approach if people actually go out and observe the process and do the detailed mapping. The reality of this approach, however, is that little if anything is usually done beyond the high-level mapping portion. It is always much easier to do high-level mapping than the real work associated with more detailed mapping efforts. As previously noted, the time devil is almost always found in the details. At a high enough mapping level, almost any process can be made to look efficient. It's not until one starts tearing a process apart that one discovers all of the time consuming waste.

Additionally, companies wishing to adopt activity-based costing (ABC) practices can easily use the collected data from Steps 2 and 3 for such purposes. This is true at both the process and associated work activity levels. Given that time and resources (e.g., number of personnel involved in a specific process or activity) have already been collected on a process analysis worksheet, one only has to know labor rates to convert all of this information into activity-related labor costs. Conversely, if annual frequencies are known, yearly activity-related costs can also be easily calculated.

The following generic case study illustrates some of the various techniques outlined in the Seven-Step PI Method, especially as they can be used at the work activity level.

CASE STUDY #1

The Custom Tooling Company, commonly referred to as CTC, fabricates highly specialized tooling for very select industry segments.

Production runs of such specialized tooling are normally quite small, usually between three and five units each. CTC has been the only major player in this niche market for years and has enjoyed an almost exclusive monopoly. As a result, the company has shown little interest in making any type of improvement to the way it does business. In fact, the existing work processes were developed years ago by the firm's founder, a respected mechanical engineer. They seem to work just fine. In CTC's entire history, there has never been any perceived incentive to improve how it does business. That is until recently, when Tooling Express abruptly appeared on the scene.

Tooling Express, it seems, can not only make specialized tooling as well as CTC, but they can do it in a quarter of the time. This speed factor offers Tooling Express a real competitive advantage in that they can charge more money for their finished products. CTC is astonished that customers are willing to pay a premium for much faster turnaround times. Alarmingly, the new upstart has already captured some 30 percent of CTC's market share.

Seriously concerned by the threat posed by Tooling Express, the president of CTC has ordered a concerted effort to reduce production cycle times. To assist in this effort, a consulting firm has been retained.

Using the Seven-Step PI Method, the consultants define the beginning of the specialized tool making process as "work order issued" and the process ending with "fabricated tooling delivered to customer." They then embark on a comprehensive process mapping initiative, although some managers within CTC think this is a waste of time. All the consultants really have to do, according to these managers, is simply sit in a comfortable conference room and let those in the know describe the process. However, the consultants insist on observing the process and actually walking out as many steps as possible. During this observation phase, they also collect time data for each identified process step. Although there are certainly some differences among the various tools fabricated, the actual process is surprisingly similar. Little actual variation is observed.

When all of the steps are mapped on a process analysis work sheet and associated step times, required resources, and costs are collected, the data is summarized and presented to top management. The top managers at CTC are amazed that their tooling fabrication process contains so many steps. "I would have never guessed," becomes a common reply. Management is especially dumbfounded by the num ber and duration of non-value-adding delays within the process. In fact, overall cycle time averages 100 days, but true value-adding time normally comprises only approximately 5 percent of that total time. Using this data, average theoretical cycle time is 100 days × 5% or 5 days. The company is currently operating on average at 20 times the oretical cycle time!

Because so many process steps have been identified (about 150 total), the consultants decide to group the steps into individual work activities. These activities, along with percent total cycle time (re member, total cycle time equals 100 days), are:

1. Work order issuance—1%

2. Production planning—24%

3. Procurement—40%

4. Receiving—5%

5. Fabrication—25%

6. Delivery— 5%

The current process at CTC works in the following general man ner. Once a work request has been received, a work order is gener ated. Because the company is already supplied with blueprints and a list of required materials from the requesting customer, this informa tion is packaged and sent on to production planning. At production planning, a bill of materials is generated and sent to procurement. In procurement, the materials are ordered. When the materials are fi nally received (normally after a lengthy delay) they are sent to receiv ing. Receiving checks to ensure that the right materials have arrived and notifies production planning. Once production planning is noti fied, they in turn notify fabrication, as well as send fabrication the blueprints and a list of materials for the requested tooling. Fabrica tion then schedules its own work internally, gets the materials from receiving, and does the work. When they've completed the job, they ship the finished tooling to delivery, who temporarily store them be fore finally shipping them on to the waiting customer.

The consultants hold a meeting with a group of CTC employees and managers representing each of the six major identified work ac-

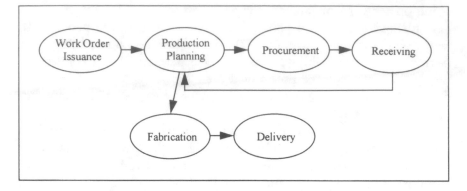

FIGURE 2.25. An initial process flow diagram at the work activity level.

tivities. They describe their findings and draw the current process flow at the activity level on a white board. This drawing is shown in Figure 2.25.

The consultants ask what is the output from each activity and list these on the white board as well. They then ask if any activities can be eliminated or combined. There is universal agreement that none can be eliminated. However, a few in the group think that some of the activities can be combined. This suggestion is quickly met with much argument and resistance by those directly affected by such changes. No one wants to possibly eliminate or combine their own work activity, even for the supposed good of the company.

After these outbursts of disagreement die down, the consultants begin to point out a few interesting observations. First, the real purpose of the process is to build custom tooling and get that tooling to the requesting customer as quickly as possible. That is the real core process. Yet in the current process, only 25 percent of the average total cycle time, at least at the activity level, is consumed with actually making what the customer wants. The bulk of the time is consumed by scheduling and procurement, which focuses on *getting* the materials, not fabricating them into a finished piece of tooling. That is, the current process at CTC is really designed for getting materials, not making custom tooling and getting them to the customer as quickly as possible.

Second, the designed process is a "push" process. That is, the process is pushed through the various activities from the beginning—

scheduling to procurement, procurement to receiving, and so on. Finally, the consultants point out that for fabrication to build a custom tool, they really need only three things: the blueprints, a list of the required materials, and the materials themselves. The blueprints and list of materials are available right at the beginning of the process. Only the materials are missing.

The consultants then ask the person from fabrication what type of process he would most like to see. The response is one in which fabrication simply gets the blueprints and materials list upfront, goes to warehousing (receiving) for the needed materials, and builds the requested tooling. It's quickly pointed out, however, from the production scheduling and procurement folks, that the materials are different for each tool. Stocking all of the different materials would be quite expensive and unnecessary. "We would never use all the materials," they insist.

The consultants point out that although this is the accepted perception at CTC, and may in fact have been true years ago when the process was originally designed, it's not true today. In fact, about 95 percent of the materials are basically the same for all tools. After digesting this information, the group collectively redesigns the process at the activity level, as shown in Figure 2.26. However, some in the room are still very resistant to any change and continuously point out why something won't work.

The newly designed process at the activity level now works like this; once a work request is made, the request is sent directly to fabrication. Fabrication immediately pulls all needed materials from warehousing. In those rare instances when materials are not immediately available, a special speed order is placed by procurement. Fabrication then schedules and builds the specialized tooling and notifies delivery, who immediately picks it up and directly ships it to the customer.

The depletion of materials in warehousing triggers procurement to reorder and replenish the consumed materials. That is, warehousing now signals procurement to replenish the used materials. This allows warehousing to keep sufficient, yet minimal, materials in stock. The replenishment of warehousing by procurement is now a separate, parallel process. It does not directly affect fabrication's cycle time. What was previously one single linear process is now two independent parallel processes; fabrication and warehouse replenishment.

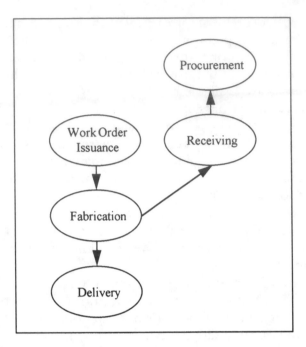

FIGURE 2.26. A redesigned process at the work activity level. Compare with Figure 2.25.

Also, the process flow path has been changed from a push to more of a pull one. Fabrication now pulls materials from warehousing. Warehousing in turn pulls materials from procurement, who in turn pulls goods from external suppliers. In addition, the activity of production planning, represented by a specific work group, has been completely eliminated. This doesn't mean, however, that no planning occurs. It's now, however, directly associated with the work.

After completing a process redesign at the activity level, the group turns its attention to the process step level previously mapped. The process steps within each remaining activity are carefully analyzed and redesigned during additional meetings. For example, numerous delay and transportation steps within the fabrication activity are eliminated by simply changing the process flow and work layout. Also, various inspection steps are combined with earlier, value-adding operation steps to form source inspections. Finished tools are also no longer temporarily stored by delivery prior to shipping. Now they are shipped immediately to the waiting customer.

What are the results of the cycle time initiative? The newly re designed process can now turn out a custom tool that is on its way to the customer in as little as 7 working days. Current average total cycle time is 9.5 days. Although there is still room for improvement, this initial cycle time effort has regained CTC's competitive position in the highly specialized tooling market. Unfortunately for a few employees and managers at CTC, the changes seem to be too much too quickly. These individuals are experiencing considerable problems in adjusting to the new way of doing business.

SUMMARY

A process typically represents the transformation and blending of a set of inputs into a more valuable set of outputs. Any process includes a series of process steps, of which there are six basic types: operation, transportation, delay, storage, inspection, and rework. Not all steps, however, add equal value to a process. Many process steps add only unnecessary delay and cost instead.

To significantly reduce cycle times, it is critical to identify non-value-adding and time consuming process waste, and then either eliminate or minimize it. As noted, speed flows from simplicity, especially simple work processes devoid of unnecessary and non-value-adding delays. Systematically identifying and eliminating such time consuming delays is a critical first step in any cycle time reduction initiative. One method for conducting such analyses is termed the Seven-Step PI Method. It includes the following steps:

1. Defining process boundaries.

2. Observing and describing process steps and flow.

3. Collect process-related data.

4. Analyze collected data.

5. Identify improvement areas.

6. Develop improvements.

7. Implement and monitor improvements.

3 ———— RESOURCE
———— AVAILABILITY

In the previous chapter, it was noted that a work process represents the transformation and blending of a set of inputs into a more valuable set of outputs. Inputs, which frequently represent various types of resources (e.g., materials, supplies, people, equipment, information), are constantly being consumed or used during this transformational process. In such instances, a process cannot move forward unless a needed resource is immediately available and accessible. When required resources are not immediately available or accessible, unnecessary delays ensue. Another key principle in cycle time reduction is assuring that the right resources are at the right place at the right time.

This resource-dependent relationship of processes is graphically illustrated in Figure 3.1. In Figure 3.1a, a five-step process consisting of three operation steps and two transportation steps is depicted graphically. Let's assume that the second operation step requires that resource x (symbolized by a hexagon) be available at time T1. If resource x is not available at time T1, a delay is created. This delay is illustrated in Figure 3.1b, which now shows a delay step occupying the position previously occupied by an operation step. Frequently, such delays caused by an unavailable resource are compounded throughout a process, greatly increasing total cycle time. A key factor then in eliminating resource-related delays is to provide the right resources when and where they're needed.

Resource-caused delays can happen for a number of reasons. Sometimes we simply don't know what the right resources are or where the right place is or what the right time is. Other times we physically don't have the right resources. That is, the right resources haven't been procured yet. Still at other times, we may have the right resources, but we can't find them or access them in a timely manner.

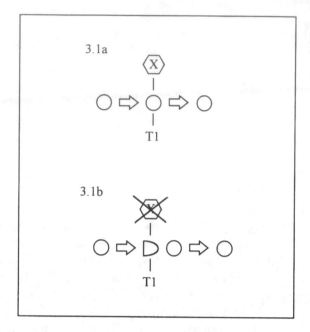

FIGURE 3.1. The unavailability of Resource X in Fig. 3.1b causes delay at time T1.

And finally, we may have the right resources and know the right place and right time, but our resource movement or logistics process is ineffective. We simply can't move required resources from point A to point B by a certain time.

Issues related to resources and resource-caused delays can be viewed from both a macro and micro perspective. We will use the term *resource availability* to refer to more macro-level issues concerning resources and their logistical movement. Resource availability refers to the degree to which resources are ready for use. If a resource is available, it is ready for use when and where needed. For example, assuring that a needed resource is moved from building A to building C and ready for use by a certain time for a specific operation step is a resource availability issue.

We can also view resources from a more micro-level view. *Resource accessibility* describes the relative ease with which resources (e.g., information, supplies, equipment, tools) can be immediately identified and retrieved within an immediate work area. Resource accessibility also refers to the ease with which an information resource, such as information on an overhead computer display, can be observed.

An example of poor resource accessibility is a service technician searching through a cluttered tool box trying to find a specific tool. Although the tool is available (it's somewhere in the tool box), it is not readily accessible. Another good example of poor accessibility is someone looking through a thick manual searching for a specific piece of information. The information is available, but it's not readily accessible. A third example is the inability to view needed information on a computer screen while performing an operation step. In this case, the needed resource cannot be easily accessed because it cannot be easily observed.

Issues associated with resource accessibility generally involve how to best organize, position, and display resources within an immediate work area. Conversely, issues associated with resource availability generally involve how to get the right resource to an immediate work environment within the right time frame in the first place.

Problems in both resource availability and resource accessibility can cause process delays. Commonly, any single delay associated with resource availability is much longer than a single delay associated with resource accessibility. However, repeated mini-delays associated with poor resource accessibility can quickly add up to significant total delay times. Therefore, it is important to focus on identifying and eliminating, or at least minimizing, delays associated with both resource availability and resource accessibility. In the following section, we will first explore issues related to resource availability.

THE THREE RESOURCE RS

For a work process to flow in a continuous manner, it is critical to have the right resources at the right place at the right time—the three resource Rs. When required resources aren't available, delays ensue and cycle times are unnecessarily increased. Although it may seem obvious, to ensure resource availability it is important to be able to answer three fundamental questions:

- What are the right resources?

- Where is the right place?

- What is the right time?

It is also important to be able to get the right resources from the "wrong" place to the right place at the right time.

In many instances, companies are unable to answer any or all three of these basic resource-related questions. They are also unable to effectively and efficiently move resources from place to place. As a result, frequent and sometimes lengthy process delays occur due to resource unavailability.

To determine the right resources required by a process, it is important to first develop a general familiarity with different resource types. Resources can be broadly grouped under the following five major categories.

- Personnel.

- Materials and supplies.

- Tools and equipment.

- Job-related information.

- External services.

Continuous work flow is normally dependent on the availability of some combination of people, materials, supplies, tools, equipment, information, and external services. Under the category of job-related information, we can also include needed decisions from varying levels of management.

In many instances, we give less forethought to the category of required job-related information than we do to the other resource categories. Yet, as more and more of us become information workers, our basic resource is information. Just as Frank Gilbreth gave considerable attention to getting bricks and mortar to his bricklayers in the most efficient manner possible, so must we become more concerned with providing available and immediately accessible information to information workers.

We can illustrate the use of these five resource categories by the following example. To successfully perform a preventive maintenance service call on a copier machine in an office setting, we need:

- A service company (external services).

- A service technician (personnel).

- Specific tools and equipment.

- Various supplies and materials.

- Information, in the form of procedures, schematics, etc.

Equipped with these major resource categories, and assuming that the proper type, quantity, and quality of each resource is correct (e.g., one properly trained technician), we have fulfilled the "right" resource part of the equation.

To create a list of the right resources for a process, it is important to understand at least three things. First, we must fully understand the process—what is to be done and what resources are required to fully support each work activity and process steps within that particular activity. Without first knowing the details of what is to be done, it is difficult if not impossible to accurately determine what resources are required.

Second, we need to understand the physical environment in which the work activity will occur. Then we must decide what additional, if any, resources are required to successfully operate in that particular physical environment. For example, because of expected climatic conditions, we may need special protective clothing for personnel or special coverings for equipment. Understanding the physical environment of the process is sometimes just as important in selecting the right resources as understanding the details of the work process itself.

Finally, we need some idea of the probability of unexpected resource needs. Given our understanding of the process, there is a probability, although not a certainty, that we may also require resources x, y, and z. For example, in the servicing of copier machines, it is unrealistic to carry all possible supplies and parts to the job site. But we may be able to determine what supplies and parts have a high probability of being needed, and either carry or position these resources accordingly. This probability-based, resource contingency planning approach will be discussed later in this chapter.

Once we understand the process, the physical environment, and probability-based resource needs, we can specifically identify the type, quality, and quantity of required resources. In essence, a resource needs analysis has been conducted. Armed with the above information, we can say we need three of resource a of specification x, four of resource b of specification y, and so on. Such resource descriptions can apply to both human and nonhuman resources. Conducting a resource analysis will be covered more fully in Chapter 7.

It is also important to include things like usability, appropriateness, quantity, and quality in our definition of right resource. A right resource is not only one that is at the right place at the right time, but is also usable, is appropriate for the required activity or step, and is of sufficient quality and quantity.

Once we have answered the "What are the right resources?" question, we can proceed to the "Where is the right place?" and "What is the right time?" questions. These two questions can only be answered correctly if we fully understand the process. Just as the first cycle time reduction principle of eliminating process waste depends on fully describing and understanding the process, so does the second principle of assuring that the right resources are at the right place at the right time.

By understanding a process, we can frequently identify a place and time with each process step, as well as what resources are required for that step. This identified resource need, place, and time process-step association is graphically illustrated in Figure 3.2. As depicted, each identified process step has an associated resource, place, and time.

In some instances, it may be impossible to create an exact process time line. Instead, only a relative time line can be created. That is, depending on such things as encountered environmental conditions and alternative process flow paths, we can only determine relative times. For example, we may only be able to determine that time T1, which is associated with process step #1, occurs before time T2, which is associated with process step #2, and so on. Even this information can prove useful, because we can now at least associate an actual process step and resource need within a relative time frame. Depending on process-specific circumstances, we may or may not be able to also identify a specific location with each process step.

In an ideal world, we would deal only with static process environments and fixed process sequences, places, and times. If this were the case, it would be fairly simple to always have the right resources at

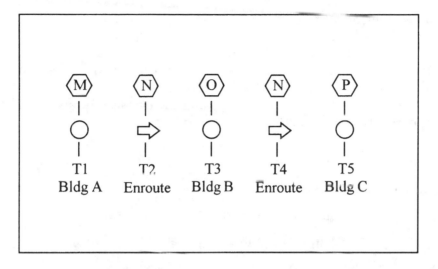

FIGURE 3.2. Combining a process step with a specific time, resource, and place.

the right place at the right time. All we would have to do is place the right resources at the right place and never worry about them again. Unfortunately, this is rarely if ever the case for at least two reasons.

First, most processes are dynamic. This means that at least something is going to change that requires moving a needed resource from one place to another. Second, processes consume and use resources that must be replenished on a periodic basis. This replenishment need also requires the movement of resources from one place to another. Therefore, we not only have to worry about determining:

- the right resources,
- the right place,
- the right time,

but we also have to concern ourselves with how to move needed resources from point A to point B by some required time.

The second basic principle of cycle time reduction then is assuring that the right resources are at the right place at the right time. This principle implies that all processes will require at least some movement of resources from point A to point B. This is especially true for such things as equipment, people, supplies, materials, services, and information. Being able to move resources to the right place at the right time in the most efficient manner possible is critical in reducing the cycle time of the total process.

To move a resource requires having the physical means to move it, plus knowing the following basic information:

- What resources (type and quantity) must be moved.

- When they must be moved by (time).

- Where they must be moved to (called the destination).

- Where they must be moved from (called the origin).

- How they must be moved (called the transportation mode).

- The most expeditious route between the origin and the destination.

Problems can occur in moving resources for a number of reasons. One commonly encountered problem is that no effective system exists for tracking the current location or origin of a resource. We may have an idea of the resource's general location, but no specific details as to its exact location. As a result, valuable time is wasted simply searching for a needed resource.

One company, for example, frequently moved specialized pieces of equipment among multiple work sites that were physically separated by various distances. Although there was a computer-based tracking system operating to identify what specialized pieces of equipment existed and in what quantity, there was no means to track the exact location of each piece of equipment. Every time a piece of equipment was needed elsewhere, someone in the transportation department had to get on the phone and begin calling to find it. This was usually a two-phase operation.

First, the general vicinity of the equipment had to be located. Once a suspected area was identified, the caller could then begin zeroing in. This second, zeroing-in task was accomplished by literally going down an alphabetical list of names until the required piece of equipment was located. Unfortunately, many people could not be immediately contacted, which multiplied the number of phone calls required.

This inefficient resource-location system caused multiple resource-related delays for the work activity that required the specialized equipment in the first place. In some instances, the equipment simply couldn't be located, which caused major delays. The company finally developed a bar-coded tracking system that eliminated this constant search-and-find activity. Instead of having to pick up the phone and make multiple calls, transportation personnel can now go to a computer screen and locate the equipment's exact whereabouts.

Another commonly encountered problem in moving required resources is that companies have overtaxed resource distribution systems. They simply don't have sufficient resources to move resources. For example, a company may not have enough trucks to move needed resources when and where they are required. At first glance, this seems like a situation where additional "moving" resources are required. Yet further examination may discover that this is not really the case at all. Trucks needed to move required resources may be tasked instead with doing non-value-adding activities. Although the trucks are being fully utilized to do something, much of that something is unnecessary. By eliminating such non-value-adding work, better value-adding resource utilization can be achieved.

A further reason companies have difficulty moving needed resources is that they may be trying to move more resources than are actually required for a specific work activity or group of activities. For example, during the Gulf War some 40,000 U.S. cargo containers of the size that tractor-trailers haul arrived in Saudi Arabia. Unfortunately, this mass of containers represented far more supplies than the Army could use, placing a severe strain on their transportation capabilities. The excess supplies not only delayed their ultimate distribution, but tied up unnecessary personnel, as well. In addition, over half of the 40,000 containers had to be opened onsite and their contents manually inventoried and relisted.

One reported reason for such excesses was overzealous supply sergeants. Supposedly, supply sergeants traditionally order three of everything, with the expectation that at least two of the requisitions will go astray in unmarked containers. If by chance all three containers show up at the right place, the resultant chaos and inefficiencies are obvious. As a result of its experience during the Gulf War, the U.S. Army is now placing sensors in each container that allows near real-time tracking via a satellite-based Global Positioning System.

The Gulf War example points out an important insight about people and resource distribution systems. When people don't trust resource distribution systems, they normally do one of two things. They either over-order needed resources, especially supplies and equipment, or hoard them with the expectation that if they ever let them go, they'll never get them back. Both situations can tax resource distribution systems, making it even more likely that process delays will result because the right resource can't be delivered to the right place at the right time.

In dealing with resource availability issues, it is important to not only know what the right resource, place, and time are, but also possess the capability to move the required resources in an efficient and effective manner. Ineffective and inefficient resource distribution systems can easily create mistrust, which frequently leads to resource hoarding or over-purchasing. Such hoarding and over-purchasing can cause time-consuming, resource-related process delays. Assuring resource availability is crucial to achieving fast cycle times.

RESOURCE ACCESSIBILITY

Although a resource may be available, it may not be immediately accessible. The right resource may be at the right place at the right time on a macro scale, but it may not be immediately accessible on a more micro level. For example, a technician may continuously interrupt an operational step to walk a few paces to retrieve a needed resource, such as a tool or piece of equipment. Knowledge or information workers continuously do the same thing, repeatedly stopping work to search for and retrieve required pieces of information. Unfortunately, these short resource retrieval sequences are rarely, if ever, identified as being part of a work process.

Retrieval sequences are usually sandwiched in between operation steps and commonly consist of:

- A transportation step, needed to reach the required resource (perhaps only a few short "human" steps).

- A delay step, composed of searching for, identifying, and then physically recovering the needed resource.

- A second transportation step, required to transport the resource back to the immediate work site.

When work is examined at such a detailed level, it is commonly comprised of operation steps interrupted by numerous resource retrieval sequences. Each miniseries is composed of an operation step and associated transportation—delay—transportation "triplet." This repetitive sequencing is illustrated in Figure 3.3. From Figure 3.3, it is easy to see how such supposedly minor interruptions can quickly add up to represent significant delays in cycle time. By eliminating or minimizing the duration of these retrieval sequences, we can often significantly reduce process cycle times.

To eliminate or minimize such micro sequences, we must improve the physical placement and spatial layout of required resources, and the organization and display of needed resources. By improving the physical placement and spatial layout of required resources, we can frequently eliminate, or at least significantly minimize, the two transportation steps associated with the three-step resource retrieval sequence. By also improving the organization and display of resources, we can minimize delays associated with searching for, identifying, and recovering a required resource.

In an ideal situation, all resources are immediately placed next to a work site within "arm's reach," such that no transportation steps are required by workers. Due to practical spatial constraints, however, this is commonly impossible. In such instances, it is often beneficial to arrange resources in some type of a layered manner about an

FIGURE 3.3. Operation steps are commonly interrupted by mini resource retrieval sequences consisting of a transportation-delay-transportation triplet.

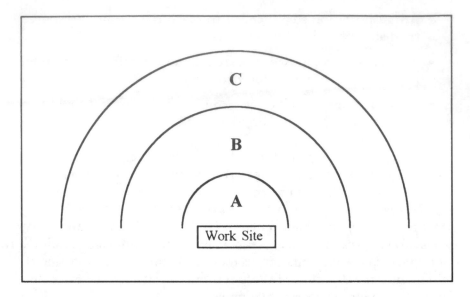

FIGURE 3.4. An example of placing resources in a layered fashion based on frequency of use. In this instance, resources found in zone A are used more frequently than resources placed in zones B or C.

operational site. One resource layout option based on frequency of use, is graphically illustrated in Figure 3.4.

In Figure 3.4, each resource layer is positioned based on its frequency of use. That is, items that are most frequently used are positioned closest to the operation site. Ideally, this most immediate or proximal resource layer is within arm's reach of a worker. Subsequent resource layers correspond to decreasing frequencies of use, with the least frequently used resources being placed in the furthest or most distal layer.

Various alternatives to this frequency-based resource layout can be employed. For example, some items may require considerable time to physically move even a short distance. This may be due to the item's weight, bulk, size, or some other parameter. In such cases, it may be advantageous to move the item closer to the immediate operation site.

Optimal resource layouts (in terms of distance from the immediate operation site) can minimize, and in some instances eliminate altogether, transportation steps associated with retrieving a needed resource. Resource layouts in respect to overall process layout will be discussed again in Chapter 5.

The organization and display of resources within a specific resource layer must be addressed next. For example, we may place a frequently used tool box within arm's length of a technician. Our next concern is how to organize the contents of the tool box so that the technician can immediately identify and easily retrieve each needed tool. What must be avoided are delays associated with having to physically search through the tool box each time a specific tool is required. Our challenge is to display needed resources in the most recognizable and identifiable manner possible, and make them physically easy to recover.

To minimize delays caused by searching for needed resources, we must first narrow the "search area" of a resource as much as possible. This narrowing effect allows individuals to immediately focus their attention in the right area. To accomplish this, we may group resources within a particular resource layer based on functional grouping. Whenever someone needs a specific resource, the search is immediately initiated in a specific resource "family" area. In grouping resources by functional groupings, each resource group contains like or similar items.

We can also group resources to parallel the temporal sequence of a process. That is, resource A is next to B which is next to C, and so on. This resource positioning corresponds to operational steps 1, 2, 3, etc. In some instances, we may wish to organize resources in some combination of functional grouping and temporal sequence. For example, we can create resource "trays" that correspond to a temporal sequence, and on each tray we can arrange resources in functional groupings.

This will allow a resource, once identified, to be easily recovered. To quickly recover a resource, the resource must be easily grasped and removed from any type of holder or container.

As noted earlier, an increasing concern for many companies is how to improve the accessibility of job-related information. Normally, because of its sheer volume, we can't display information in the same way that we can statically display a tool or other required piece of equipment. Yet, it is very important from a cycle time reduction perspective to be able to access quickly needed information resources.

In organizing information, we must create trails or pathways through an information source that quickly lead us to the specific information required. Given an information need, we must be able to quickly follow an easily recognizable "trail" to a specific information item.

In many instances, we can apply some of the same concepts just discussed to organizing information as well. For example, we can organize information under functional groupings. We can also organize it along some type of temporal process sequence. In the latter instance, if we're about to do operation Step 4, we may wish to organize information so that we can directly access Step 4, and from there immediately begin our search pattern for a specific piece of information relating to that particular step.

Computer-based information systems have much to offer for quickly accessing and displaying job-related information. Yet this potentially valuable feature of information technology has yet to be fully exploited. Earlier attempts at developing computer-based, job-specific information systems were frequently criticized as being nothing more than "fast page turners." From a cycle time perspective, however, an extremely fast page turner is exactly what's wanted. Some of the many issues associated with using technology to improve resource accessibility and availability will be explored more fully in Chapter 4.

Frequently, resource accessibility can be significantly improved simply through good housekeeping practices. Sloppy work areas can cause delays associated with searching for and retrieving a needed resource. Keeping work areas clean and orderly is an inexpensive way of immediately improving resource accessibility.

To improve resource accessibility, it is necessary to eliminate or minimize transportation times to reach a needed resource, minimize delay times to search for and identify a needed resource, as well as to physically retrieve that resource, and eliminate or minimize transportation times to transport the resource to an immediate operation site. To improve resource accessibility, we must improve the physical and spatial layout of required resources, and the organization and display of needed resources.

Although the elapsed time of any single delay accessing a required resource is usually quite small, and rarely even considered, the high frequency with which they occur quickly accumulates. Indeed, significant cumulative delay times can be attributed to poor resource accessibility. It is important, therefore, to focus on resource-related delays at both the macro and micro levels. In many instances, greater overall gains in cycle time reduction can be made at the micro level because of the very high frequencies generally involved. As mentioned earlier, the time devil is often in the details and in all of the supposedly insignificant things that we never really think about.

CONTINGENT RESOURCES

As noted throughout this chapter, a key principle in reducing cycle time is ensuring that the right resources are at the right place at the right time. This right requirement is applicable at a macro and micro level, applying to both resource availability and resource accessibility. In this section, we will briefly explore the role of resource contingency planning for unexpected resource needs. Unexpected resources are resources that are required because of unplanned equipment failures or unexpectedly encountered process conditions or problems.

In almost all processes, we can identify resources that are absolutely required to move a process forward. For example, if we are producing output X which is comprised of a special blend of ingredients, then it is essential to have those ingredients (resources) available at the right time and place. In such instances, a well-defined relationship exists between an output and a set of required resource inputs. Without these specific resource inputs, no output is possible and the process cannot move forward.

A somewhat less defined relationship can also exist. It may be unknown if a resource is definitely needed to move a process forward, but there is a high probability that it will be required to do so. That is, there is a very high probability that a specific condition will be encountered or a particular need will arise that requires a specific resource if the process is to continue moving forward. This high probability category frequently applies to resources like supplies, materials, equipment, and information.

For example, service technicians sent to conduct routine preventive maintenance on office equipment may not know for sure exactly what parts will need replacing, if any. Yet, past experience suggests that parts A and B have a high probability of needing replacement.

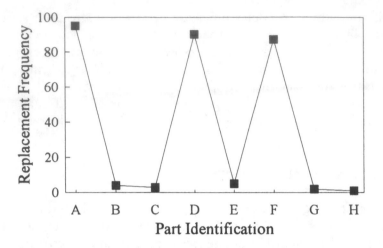

FIGURE 3.5. A frequency line graph depicting replacement frequencies of various parts.

Therefore, it's prudent to carry these specific parts to the job site, because not having them will cause an unnecessary, and in this case, avoidable (from a probability viewpoint) delay.

Such high-probability resources can frequently be identified by constructing simple frequency distribution charts. For example, Figure 3.5 illustrates the frequency in which eight different parts require replacing during routine service calls. It's obvious from the graph that parts A, D, and F have a very high probability of being replaced on such calls. It makes sense then for service technicians to carry at least these three parts with them on all service calls. On the basis of cost, space availability, and other considerations, however, carrying the other five parts on a routine basis may not be warranted.

From this short examination, two broad categories of resources can be identified. The first category represents resources that are known to be needed. That is, there is an absolute certainty that they will be consumed or used during a given process or work activity. Such resources are simply a part of the required process inputs. Without them, the process cannot move forward.

A second broad resource category can also be identified based on a high probability of need. These resources have a very high probability, although not certainty, that they will be required to move a process forward. It is suggested that these high probability resources should also be made available and easily accessible during any process or work activity.

There is also a third broad category of resources termed *low-probability* resources. Low-probability resources are resources that are required only on a very infrequent or periodic basis. They are usually needed due to unplanned equipment failures or unexpectedly encountered process conditions or problems. Unfortunately, this low-probability resource category is frequently very difficult to identify. Only through the generation of a number of "what-if" scenarios, can such resources be adequately identified.

If low-probability resources are needed and are not immediately available or accessible, lengthy process delays could possibly ensue. However, it is usually unrealistic to have all imaginable resources immediately available and accessible at any work site. Cost, space, transportability, as well as many other factors, represent real barriers to having every conceivable, low-probability resource immediately available and accessible. Therefore, a real dilemma is created. Without such resources, delays may be created that significantly lengthen cycle time. Yet, due to such things as cost, space, and transportability, it is frequently impractical to always have such resources available.

One avenue in dealing with this dilemma is to develop contingency plans for acquiring low-probability resources in as expedient a manner as possible. For example, one company periodically required special services of a highly unique and technical nature. It made little economical sense, however, to have such capabilities in-house and immediately available at all times. There just wasn't sufficient demand to justify the high associated costs. Instead, the company developed a well-prepared contingency plan so that a system was already in place to expedite required services where they were needed. In this instance, the company was willing to accept a short resource-caused delay, yet had developed sufficient contingency plans to minimize the extent of the delay. In many instances, upfront resource contingency planning can significantly minimize delays associated with unexpected, low-probability resource needs.

Another approach in dealing with low-probability resource requirements is to use a risk-based approach. Risk is defined as *Probability × Consequences*. In some instances, although the probability of needing a specific resource is quite low, the consequences associated with not having that resource may be unacceptable from a business standpoint. A delay of such proportion may result that the company could lose significant money or some other competitive advantage. Therefore, it may make sense to have the resource immediately available and accessible, even though a high probability exists that it may never be used.

For example, a summer field party exploring for precious minerals in a remote region of the Arctic may have a very low probability of needing a specific piece of equipment. Yet, if the need should arise and the equipment is not immediately available, the field party may experience a prolonged delay, seriously jeopardizing the success of the seasonal effort. Therefore, it may make sense, if practical, to transport the piece of equipment to the field. In another, less remote setting, however, the consequences may be much less because the equipment can quickly be supplied on an as-needed basis.

A resource-based risk matrix can be a useful method for identifying low probability, yet high consequence resources. A resource-based matrix identifies the type of resource, the probability of it being required in order to move a process forward, and the consequences associated with not having the resource immediately available.

In Table 3.1, resource C has a low probability of being needed to move a process forward. Yet, it has also been identified as having a

TABLE 3.1. RESOURCE PROBABILITY MATRIX

Resource	Associated Process Step	100% Probability	Very High Probability	Low Probability, High Consequence
A	#1	X		
B	#3	X		
C	#3			X
D	#6	X		
E	#6		X	
F	#8	X		

high-consequence factor if it is needed and not immediately available. That is, if resource C should be needed and is not present, lengthy and possibly unacceptable delays could result. In such instances, a decision must be made as to whether to acquire the resource and have it immediately available, or have some other contingency plan in place.

Resources can be grouped under three broad categories based on probability of need:

- Those resources that have a 100% probability of being needed to move a process forward.

- Those resources that have a high probability of being needed to move a process forward.

- Those resources that have a low probability of being needed during a process. Low-probability resources, however, may have associated high consequences, such as unacceptable delays, if they should be needed and are not immediately available.

Identifying these three resource categories can be very important in eliminating or minimizing resource related delays. By categorizing resources based on their probability of need and associated consequences, informed decisions can be made regarding resource acquisition and alternative resource contingency plans. Although contingency plans may not be able to eliminate all delays caused by unavailable resources, they can significantly minimize those delays.

In the following generic case study, some of the important concepts of resource availability and accessibility will be illustrated. The importance of identifying contingent resources will also be portrayed.

CASE STUDY #2

LabQuip is a major manufacturer of sophisticated laboratory equipment. The company does not sell its equipment outright, however. Rather, it leases its laboratory equipment to various government, university, private, and hospital-related laboratories. With the lease comes a standard, fixed-priced service contract.

Competition in the sale of such technologically sophisticated laboratory equipment is fairly intense. There are two other major players that LabQuip continuously competes against. These three companies currently control about 90 percent of the market, divided almost equally among themselves. The three major rivals routinely compete on the quality, lease price, and associated features of their equipment. This latter features category keeps the company's design engineers in a constant frenzy trying to develop yet another new feature.

To assist the engineers in identifying features wanted by customers, the marketing group sent out a detailed questionnaire to all of its current and potential customers. When the questionnaires were returned, however, upper management was astonished. Instead of wanting more additional features, what customers really wanted was better service. Specifically, customers wanted the following:

- Equipment that was highly reliable. "We just want to turn the equipment on and it keeps running continuously," stated one customer.

- No unscheduled breakdowns. "We run this stuff 24 hours a day, seven days a week. It can't break down. When it does, it costs us a fortune," replied another customer.

- Extremely fast preventive maintenance (PM) service calls. "Time is money. Every minute counts. The longer you take in doing PMs, the more money we lose. Learn to do them in about half the time," demanded one major customer.

LabQuip was amazed at these survey findings. Although, in the past, they and their competition have tried to differentiate themselves solely on the quality and price of their equipment, LabQuip realized that they can also differentiate themselves on the speed of the service they provide their customers. That is, they can offer high-quality equipment, competitive lease prices, *and* extremely fast service.

A small task team was put together to significantly reduce the cycle time associated with doing service PMs. The team's goal, given to them by the president of LabQuip, was to reduce PM service cycle time by at least a third. Using the Seven-Step PI Method presented in Chapter 2, the group began to observe and map a number of service calls made by the company's field technicians. They determined from the collected process analysis worksheets that the average service call, measured by the amount of time the customer's laboratory equipment is actually offline, is about two hours or 120 minutes. Value-added steps, however, accounted for only 20 percent of this total cycle time. Theoretical cycle time then is 20% x 120 minutes or 24 minutes. After discovering this information, the team set a new goal for itself of reducing service PM cycle times by 75 percent to only 30 minutes.

Two types of process flow diagrams were then created from the process analysis worksheets. Initially, they were developed at a fairly high level. The first high-level process flow diagram created was for the laboratory equipment receiving the PM itself. It began from the time the equipment was initially taken out of service to the time it was placed back in operation and running again. This object- or equipment-oriented process flow diagram looks like this.

$$D\ O\ D\ O\ D\ O\ D$$

A delay in the PM process represents times when the technician was physically not working on the equipment or when the equipment was sitting idly and nothing was physically being done to it.

The task team then focused its attention on the actions of the service technicians themselves. They first used the same higher level approach. This task-focused, higher-level process flow perspective looks like this.

$$O\ \Rightarrow\ D\ \Rightarrow\ O\ \Rightarrow\ D\ \Rightarrow\ O\ \square$$

Numerous non-value-adding delays and transportation steps were identified. The team then took the higher level process flow diagram depicting the service technicians and performed a micro level analysis of the various operation steps. This more detailed analysis is shown here.

$$O\ \Rightarrow\ D\ \Rightarrow\ O\ \Rightarrow\ D\ \Rightarrow\ O\ \Rightarrow\ D\ \Rightarrow\ O$$

The same pattern of delays and transportation steps noted at the macro level is also observed at the micro level.

The team then began to look at the reason for the delays and associated transportation steps at both the macro and micro levels and found that most of the delays and transportation steps were associated with finding and retrieving required resources. Technicians were being delayed at the macro level by having to stop work and walk to their service vans to retrieve a needed resource. They were also incurring numerous mini-delays at the micro level by having to stop an operation step and walk a few steps to search for and retrieve a needed resource, such as a specific tool or piece of information.

A pie chart of the types of resources retrieved at the macro level was constructed next. As shown in Figure 3.6, technicians were mostly seeking supplies (mainly parts), information, and tools and test equipment. All of these materials are usually stored haphazardly in a technician's service van, parked some distance from the immediate job site. At the macro level then, delays are caused during the preventive maintenance process by technicians having to stop work and walk to their service vans to get needed items or retrieve needed information.

On a micro level, it is the same story. Technicians were experiencing numerous delays having to sort through poorly organized tool boxes or search for required information in poorly organized service

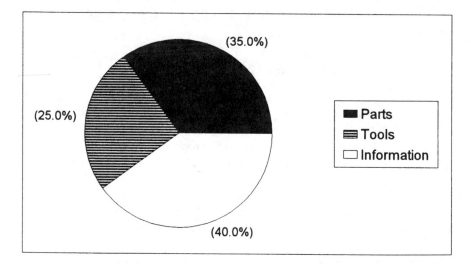

FIGURE 3.6. A pie chart depicting the frequency of various resource types.

manuals. The task team realized that its first major goal was to create more immediate access to required resources. They divided the resource types into three broad categories:

- Parts and supplies.

- Tools and test equipment.

- Information.

The team first focused on parts and supply resource requirements. Service technicians, the team discovered, routinely service different models of the *same* piece of equipment. For example, they routinely service models 100, 200, 300, and 300X of the Mark VII. Parts and supplies for all models are commonly stored (more like heaped or dumped) together in a large box in each technician's service van.

A frequency chart for each model was constructed showing typically replaced parts and needed supplies. A frequency chart showing the frequency of replaced parts for a model 200 Mark VII is shown in Figure 3.7. Two things are evident. First, each model routinely requires different supplies and the replacement of different parts. That

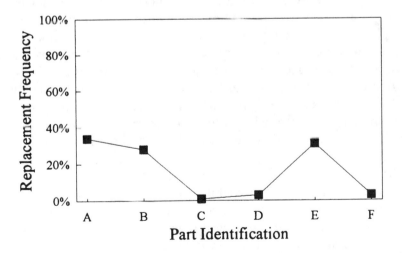

FIGURE 3.7. A frequency line graph depicting replacement frequencies of various parts.

is, required parts and supplies for a Model 100 are different from a Model 200, and so on. Second, only a few parts are routinely replaced within each model. In fact, about 97 percent of the time, only three parts are replaced in each model. However, these common parts differ from model to model.

Armed with this information, the team developed easily identifiable and transportable supply and part kits for each model. These supply and part kits are now carried directly to the immediate job site prior to starting the PM. Individual parts and supplies are no longer left in the service van for retrieval during the PM process itself.

Next, required tools and test equipment were analyzed. Although some differences in tools and test equipment required for each model were identified, the differences were slight. The team, therefore, decided to focus its efforts on creating highly organized and easily accessible tool displays. Tools are now organized by functional groupings, each with a permanent and easily identifiable place. They are also spatially placed based on frequency of use to maximize accessibility. Also, initial drawings of a special stand were created to better hold, display, and position the most frequently used tools. Stands for the test equipment were also developed.

Finally, the information resource problem was tackled. A number of different paper-based information systems were suggested, but all had significant drawbacks. Team members convinced themselves that a computer-based system was needed instead. Required information, complete with schematics, were placed on a notebook computer. The stand that was originally developed to support the tool box was redesigned to also accommodate the notebook computer. With the newly designed stand, tools and information are now immediately accessible to the service technicians. By implementing these three related improvements, much of the resource-related delays at both the macro- and micro-level were either eliminated or significantly minimized.

One other significant improvement was also made, unrelated to resource availability and accessibility. Prior to redesigning the service PM process flow, technicians would routinely take the laboratory equipment offline before setting up. This shutdown caused a significant and completely unnecessary delay at the very beginning of the PM process itself. However, as discovered in the manufacturing sector, much initial preparation can normally be undertaken *before* taking equipment offline. The same principle was applied here. In the newly redesigned process, the technicians keep the laboratory equipment up and running while setting up. Only when they are completely ready, do they take the equipment offline. This simple improvement alone saved considerable laboratory downtime.

In the end, the team closely met their self-imposed target of reducing cycle time by 75 percent. Management and affected customers were quite pleased and rather astonished. As a result of this drastic improvement, some "perspective" customers became real ones.

It is important to note that throughout this cycle time reduction initiative, the assigned improvement team worked closely with the effected technicians. Indeed, technicians were physically represented on the team itself. As a result of the team's efforts, the technicians received a big boost in perceived status within the company. In fact, the technicians have become the new "hot shots" of the company, taking a great deal of pride in how quickly and effectively they can perform preventive maintenance calls.

Summary

A second key principle in cycle time reduction is providing the right resources at the right place and the right time. Resource-related delays can be caused by not having resources available when and where they are needed. They can also be caused by not having resources immediately accessible and reachable. Issues associated with resource availability generally involve how to get the right resource to a work environment (the right place) at the right time. Similarly, issues relating to resource accessibility generally involve how to best place, organize, and display resources within an immediate work setting.

Any single delay caused by an unavailable resource is usually much longer than a single delay associated with an inaccessible resource. However, repeated mini-delays associated with poor resource accessibility can quickly add up to significant total delay times. It is important, therefore, to focus on identifying and eliminating, or at least minimizing, delays associated with both resource availability and resource accessibility.

4 —— SPEED AND
—— TECHNOLOGY

The first two basic principles of cycle time reduction involve eliminating process waste and providing the right resources at the right place and time. In this chapter, we'll explore the third basic principle of cycle time reduction—using technology to improve process flow. Just as Frank Gilbreth redesigned the scaffolding used by his workers to increase the speed and ease of laying bricks, we can use technology, especially computer-based information and communications technologies, to significantly increase the efficiencies of modern day work processes. Indeed, quantum leaps in reducing cycle times may be made possible by the successful application of many new emerging technologies, such as wireless mobile technologies.

For many, it seems that we are currently experiencing an almost unprecedented state of technological change and growth. The fields of medicine, transportation, communication, manufacturing, and engineering, to name only a few, have greatly benefited from advancements and applications of new technologies. Some would even argue that the future growth and potential use of new technologies are almost limitless, capable of fundamentally changing the way we work. Such fundamental changes are especially needed if we are to more rapidly acquire, transform, distribute, and apply information. Currently, information-related tasks account for 40 to 60 percent of an average worker's time, 20 to 40 percent of typical labor costs, and 12 to 15 percent of corporate revenues.

Some of the technological changes that we are currently witnessing represent evolutionary advances in existing technologies. Others, however, may well represent quantum revolutionary leaps. This evolutionary versus revolutionary pace of change is perhaps best illustrated in the field of computer interface technology[1]. Bigger displays, improved simulations, and better graphics all represent evolutionary changes associated with the development of computer interfaces. Artificial intelligence technologies such as user intent recognition and context-sensitive aiding; user interface technologies represented by virtual reality, multimedia, and true three-dimensional displays; and system technologies, illustrated by object-oriented programming techniques and high-performance communications, may well possess the potential to revolutionize many information-intensive work environments. Indeed, in these latter examples, it really does seem that the boundaries of technological design are almost limitless.

One company, for example, found that the application of information and factory-automation technology could give it an edge in the highly competitive furniture manufacturing industry. At one of its plants, the company installed computer-controlled equipment that uses lasers to cut and lay fabric for upholstered furniture. The new machinery can match patterns with surgical, to-the-millimeter precision. It can also be programmed to produce chairs, sofas, and love seats on a single production line. Installation of the new technology has reportedly decreased inventory cycle times by some 25 percent.

Yet, for all of the glowing predictions and futuristic visions associated with pending technological advancements, there is also a littered trail of broken promises, half-truths, and costly experiments. Many emerging technologies, for example, are touted as some magical panacea capable of solving most, if not all, of our collective problems. Unfortunately, such unrealistic predictions rarely live up to their full billing, leaving behind instead a disgruntled and skeptical populace.

These two, very opposite views of technology are especially relevant in cycle time reduction. Technology can be a powerful ally in any cycle time reduction initiative, yet, when improperly applied, the same technology can quickly become an expensive and time-consuming hindrance.

When we explore the role of technology in cycle time reduction, three key points emerge.

Technology can place real constraints on any cycle time reduction initiative. In many instances, technology places physical and temporal constraints on cycle times. For example, trying to decrease the cycle time of loading and unloading passengers on a commercial jet is constrained by the fact that hundreds of people must be moved through a single door. No matter what you do, unless you totally redesign the whole system, you must still confront the physical limitations placed by that one single door.

A specific capacity limitation is another example of a technological constraint. A given technology can only do whatever it does just so fast. For example, a photocopier machine can only make so many copies per minute. This number represents a physical constraint that must be dealt with to decrease the cycle time of a process using this particular copier. Therefore, the design of a specific technology frequently limits the number and type of improvement alternatives.

Technology is basically neutral—it's how we use it that counts. In many instances, we can use technology to significantly decrease cycle times. In other instances, however, inappropriate applications of the exact same technology can actually increase cycle times.

E-mail systems are a good example of how the exact same technology can be used in both positive and negative ways. One university, for example, wanted very much to join the information highway. The university offers various graduate programs via long distance. They further use a network of student advisers located throughout the country to augment a small, full-time faculty staff. The primary role of the advisers is to serve on or chair student committees involving a terminal program project. In the course of their work, advisers routinely call the home campus to exchange information and coordinate various student-related activities.

The university sought to eliminate these calls by using an electronic mail system. Both advisers and full-time faculty members at the campus were instructed to post messages and questions on an electronic bulletin board. However, for economic reasons, advisers couldn't log on to the electronic mail system until nighttime. Once logged on, advisers read their messages and responded accordingly, or sent new messages of their own. In some instances, two or three message exchanges have to occur before a student-related matter can be completely resolved. What used to take only a few minutes by telephone can now take up to three or four days by E-mail. Such inefficiencies cause considerable coordination problems for advisers and students, as well as decrease customer (student) response times. In this example, the inappropriate use of a new technology actually lengthened cycle time.

In another example, an employee revised a company policy directive and sent it out for review and concurrence over the company's E-mail system. The employee sent it to three people simultaneously. Each person reviewed the suggested changes and either concurred with them or made minor changes. They then sent their comments back to the employee. She then incorporated all of the comments and sent the document out a second time for final concurrence. All three people sent their concurrences back to her. What would have normally taken several days in a traditional paper and mail delivery system, now takes only a few hours electronically. In this example, a specific technology was used to great advantage to decrease cycle time.

Always start with understanding the process first, then apply a specific technology to improve that process. In many instances, we just do things backwards. We purchase a piece of technology (with no idea of exactly what we're going to use it for) and then try to build a process around it. Or even worse, we try to use a piece of technology with little or no thought as to its real process function. Without first fully understanding a work process, it's almost impossible to intelligently identify and implement a supporting technology.

For example, simply computerizing a slow paper-based process with little process forethought usually results in a slow computer-based process with no significant reduction in cycle time. All that has really been done is an exchange of one presentation medium for another. Nothing has been done to change the process itself. The key in using technology to reduce cycle time is to always have the technology serve a specific, value-adding, process-related function.

In reviewing the merits of any technology, it is always wise to ask what is the real function of the technology and how can it specifically be used to reduce cycle time. Simply asking this question can provide some very valuable insights.

Technology, from a cycle time perspective, can basically serve the following five different functions. It can:

- Eliminate various steps from a process.

- Minimize the time associated with various process steps.

- Combine two or more process steps.

- Improve resource availability.

- Improve resource accessibility.

In the following sections, each of these potential process functions will be explored.

PROCESS STEP ELIMINATION

In some instances, technology can be used to eliminate a process step or sequence of steps. As described in Chapter 2, eliminating one process step often means eliminating other additional steps as well. Given a specific process flow (such as illustrated in the following process flow diagram), how can a particular technology be applied to eliminate a specific process step or sequence of steps?

$$\text{OD} \Rightarrow \text{DOD} \Rightarrow \text{DO} \square \Rightarrow \triangledown$$

To answer this question, two things must be known. What is the current process flow, and how will a particular technology specifically improve that flow? It is crucial to start with understanding the process first and determining what specific process improvements are needed, before identifying a supporting technology.

For example, a small company publishes an industry newsletter on a weekly basis. They use a desktop publishing system for their weekly publication. Although they like to include photographs in the newsletter, this is often a very time-consuming process. First the photograph must be taken, then the film has to be developed and pictures printed. After the prints have dried, they have to be scanned into a computer, where they are retouched using a software program before being placed into the newsletter. Because of the time the current process takes, the company explored alternative technologies that might help them rapidly incorporate photos into their newsletter.

After understanding the current process and the limitations of traditional film development, the company investigated using a digital camera instead of its current 35mm format. They realized that with a digital camera, they can completely eliminate the following steps:

1. Develop film.

2. Print pictures.

3. Scan photos into computer.

By using a digital camera, they can take a digitized picture and then directly upload that picture into their desktop publishing software program.

The company was concerned, however, that such time savings may be offset by a reduction in photo quality. Trial test results indicated that the loss in quality is minor compared to the significant savings in time. The company decided to purchase the digital camera and began using it in the publication of its weekly newsletter. In this example, a new technology was used to eliminate a series of process steps, thereby significantly decreasing associated cycle time.

A similar potential reduction in cycle time can be made in some situations with the use of hand-held or palm-top computers. Such small computers are sometimes referred to as Personal Digital Assistants or PDAs. Frequently, inspectors, nurses, field scientists, sampling crews, inventory personnel, as well as many others collect data in a paper format on a clipboard while working. Once the data is collected, they or someone else later enter it into a computer. After entering the data, some type of quality inspection is frequently done to assure that no transcription errors have been made while transferring the data from a paper to electronic format.

A simplified process flow diagram of this activity looks something like this.

$$\bigcirc\ \circledR\ \square$$

The flow diagram indicates that collecting the initial data in the field represents an operation step. Entering the collected data into the computer, however, actually represents a rework step. The same data has already been recorded in a paper format once before. The real purpose of the inspection step then is to inspect the quality of a rework step. Of the three-step sequence—operation, rework, and inspection—only the operation step is directly adding value. The other two steps are simply lengthening the cycle time of this information recording activity.

By redesigning the process such that the data is directly entered into a PDA when it is initially collected, both the rework step (having to enter the data into a computer) and the inspection step (reviewing the entered data) are eliminated. Now the data has to be collected only once at its source and then directly uploaded into a computer. This method not only saves considerable time by eliminating both an unnecessary rework and inspection step, but also eliminates the possibility that some type of transcription error will be made and not caught. In this instance, a specific technology, a PDA, has been selected to eliminate two process steps—a rework step and an inspection step.

MINIMIZE TIME DURATIONS

In many instances, we cannot entirely eliminate a step from a process. However, we can frequently minimize the time associated with such steps. In this regard, technology can be an extremely useful ally. In the following process flow diagram, for example, we may not be able to eliminate all of the transportation steps. However, we may be able to minimize the times associated with these steps.

$$O D \Rightarrow D O \Rightarrow$$

If the transportation steps involve moving information, we can use a number of alternative technologies. These may include sending the information via fax or a direct computer modem link-up. Since we directly add value to information only when we're using it—and not sending it—it's important to minimize all non value-adding steps like sending information as much as possible.

We can also use alternative technologies to transport goods to market more quickly. One air cargo company recognized that more demanding global consumers are changing manufacturing and retailing by forcing ever-shorter product cycle times[3]. The company capitalized on this speed need by offering "time-definite services." Time-definite service is the airfreight's equivalent to manufacturing's just-in-time concept. It basically represents a flying warehouse that delivers cargo to customer-chosen destinations exactly when it is wanted. This door-to-door service eliminates time consuming handling and storage delays and greatly increases schedule reliability.

Time-definite service works something like this. A front-end loading 747 jumbo jet leaves Hong Kong in the early morning with a load of men's suits. The suits are pressed, placed on a hanger, priced (with appropriate store tags), and hung on racks. The plane arrives that same afternoon at its destination (say, New York). The suits are unloaded and transported directly to the sales floor, ready for customer purchase the next morning.

What used to take six weeks transit time during shipment now takes only a couple of days. By selecting an alternative transportation mode and technology (plane vs. ship), goods can be made available to customers in a fraction of the time. In fast moving industries like the garment industry, such time savings represent a very significant competitive advantage. As pointed out by Harry Peterson[4] of Alfred University, such transportation time savings can also represent real bottom-line cost savings to a company.

According to Peterson, companies that try to decrease transportation costs by selecting slower, and therefore cheaper, modes of transportation may actually be increasing their associated overall business costs, as well as unnecessarily lengthening customer service response times. Peterson presents an interesting example to illustrate this "penny-wise-but-pound-foolish" condition.

A manufacturing company regularly imports goods from overseas. To supposedly cut transportation costs, the company ships the goods by ocean freighter instead of air freighting them. However, this slower transportation method normally takes two to three weeks. This includes moving the goods from the country of origin, getting them through customs, and finally transporting them overland to the company's warehouse. Because of the variabilities in transportation times and resultant unreliable arrival schedules, the company must waste capital to maintain a large warehouse buffer stock. In addition, the company must also maintain a large dollar investment in its "pipeline" inventory, represented by goods owned but unavailable while in transit.

Further, the selected transport method costs the company additional funds due to high loss and damage, as well as associated packaging and handling costs. What appears to be a cheap transportation savings is actually a costly waste of working capital. In this instance, paying more for a faster transportation mode, thereby minimizing associated transportation times, would actually save the company real working capital that can be better leveraged elsewhere.

Technology can also be used to minimize delay steps associated with a work process. This is especially true for delay steps in searching for job-specific information. One company, for example, operated a hazardous waste site for the government. In case of an emergency, the company has 15 minutes to categorize the emergency before notifying the required officials and taking the appropriate protective actions. Depending on the classification category, different officials are notified and different actions are taken. Also, depending on the time of day, different people have responsibility for categorizing an emergency.

A bulky and very user-unfriendly procedure is used to assist in this emergency categorization process. The procedure consists of a long list of "if-then" rules contained in a decision tree matrix format. A typical rule might be, *IF greater than 500 gallons of chemical X is present, THEN go to page 7 and continue with question #23. IF not, THEN continue with question #8.* If someone is unable to categorize the emergency within the allotted 15-minute time frame (which is frequently the case) the person automatically defaults to the highest emergency level. Unfortunately, in many cases this categorization is unwarranted and needlessly expensive.

An employee is tasked with decreasing the cycle time associated with categorizing an emergency. The employee first observes various individuals practicing categorizations during simulated emergencies. He records these observations on a process analysis worksheet, noting that most of the time is spent flipping through pages searching for the next appropriate question. This repetitive answer-a-question (an operation step) and search-for-next-question (a delay step) minisequence looks something like this.

$$\triangleright \; O \triangleright \; O \triangleright \; O \triangleright \; O \triangleright \; O \triangleright$$

From these observations, it is realized that very little time (less than 10 percent) is actually spent in answering questions. That is, true value-adding time is minimal and most of the time is spent in searching for the next question. What is needed to reduce cycle time is a means to minimize all of the delays associated with flipping pages.

The employee reformats the questions and develops a simple computer-based decision aid consisting of branching yes-or-no questions. No content changes are actually made to the questions, however. The question content remains exactly the same, only the format and presentation medium is changed. Now depending on a specific response to a question, the new computer program automatically branches to the next appropriate question. This rapid presentation method saves the user from having to manually flip through multiple pages to find the next appropriate question.

To test out the newly created computer-based decision aid, the employee develops a rather complex accident scenario. He then divides a group of people who are routinely tasked with making emergency categorizations into two groups. The first group makes the categorization using the traditional paper procedure with categorization times ranging between 14 and 17 minutes. Interestingly, most people in this group simply default to the highest classification category. He then has the second group use the computer version. Categorization times range between 75 and 90 seconds. After this successful demonstration, the company adopts the new computer-based version. The software program is loaded on notebook computers and placed in vehicles used by personnel who respond to an emergency and are tasked with making a categorization.

What's interesting about this example is that the actual operation of categorizing an emergency has not changed. That is, the computer does not make the decision, the human still does. What the computer does do, however, is greatly minimize the non-value-adding time associated with flipping through multiple pages. In this sense, the computer represents a very fast page turner. It also represents an excellent application of using a specific technology to reduce response cycle time in an emergency situation.

COMBINE PROCESS STEPS

Besides eliminating and minimizing process steps, technology can often allow us to combine various process steps. A common example of this ability is a copier machine that not only makes photocopies, but also sorts and staples the copied materials. In this case, the copier combines three operation steps—photocopying, sorting, and stapling—into one continuous activity. Some copiers will also perform a type of self-inspection, such as detecting when the toner is low. The copier can then either indicate the low toner situation with warning lights or add more toner automatically.

This latter example illustrates the ability to technologically combine an operation step with an inspection step. As noted in Chapter 2, processes normally entail various inspections. A normal operation and inspection sequence usually looks something like this.

That is, after an operation step, an object may be moved somewhere else for an inspection. Such inspections are often accompanied by a preceding delay step. However, if a defect is found during the inspection, rework is normally undertaken to remedy the defect. An additional inspection following the rework is frequently required as well. This operation-inspection-rework-inspection sequence may look something like this when all associated transportation and delay steps are included.

$$\bigcirc \Rightarrow \triangleright \square \triangleright \Rightarrow \triangleright \circledR \Rightarrow \triangleright \square$$

Such process flows have two inherent problems. First, they lengthen process cycle times because of the extra delay and transportation steps associated with inspections and any rework that may be required. Second, the defect may continue to be repeated until the defect is identified during an inspection step, and the source or cause of the defect is resolved.

In many instances, this process flow sequence can be compressed and defects instantly identified by performing the inspection right at the source of the operation by combining an operation step with an inspection step. As noted in Chapter 2, such inspections are called source inspections.

Sometimes technology can greatly aid in conducting source inspections. In a manufacturing setting, for example, machines can be fitted with intelligent sensors that add an inspection step to an operation step. If the sensors detect a defect, the machine stops automatically, preventing the continued manufacturing of a defective part or product. The Japanese call this feature *jidohka* or *autonomation* (not to be confused with automation). Autonomation is a word used to describe machines that are designed to stop automatically whenever a problem occurs. The use of autonomation has greatly changed manufacturing in Japan and elsewhere by allowing workers to attend multiple machines. By using autonomation, workers no longer have to attend machines when they are functioning normally. They now only have to attend to machines when they have stopped and require adjustment or repair thereby increasing resource utilization of the workers themselves.

We can apply this same concept to other work environments, as well. We can design software programs that will only accept data within a predetermined and defined set of parameters. If we try to enter something outside of these predefined parameters, it won't be accepted. For example, a predetermined range of a human's temperature may be defined in a patient charting software program. A nurse entering a patient's temperature into the program would be unable to enter any number such as 141.4, outside of this predetermined range.

It is important when evaluating technology from a cycle time perspective to ascertain if a specific technology can be used to combine various process steps. We also should determine if technology can be developed to prevent an error from occurring in the first place, thus preventing time-consuming rework. Increasingly, the challenge in technology development is to create technologies that can combine various process functions into a one-stop shop.

RESOURCE AVAILABILITY

Besides using technology whenever possible to eliminate, minimize, or combine process steps, thereby reducing cycle times, we can also use technology to aid in improving resource availability as well. Through thoughtful technological design, we can sometimes even eliminate the need for required external resources altogether. This latter condition is well illustrated by the new C-17 Globemaster III cargo jet, developed by McDonnell Douglas.

The C-17 is wide-bodied and sits low to the ground. These design characteristics greatly facilitate the loading and unloading of cargo. Also, loading is made faster with an easy roll-on, roll-off system embedded in the floor of the cargo hold which eliminates the need for unique ground support equipment. That is, the right resources no longer have to be at the right place and right time because they're basically designed into the plane itself. They're always at the right place and time! This built-in resource capability prevents potential cycle time delays caused by resource unavailability (i.e., lack of ground support equipment). Eliminating such potential delays is especially important when having to unload military cargo under hostile battle conditions.

We can use technology to improve resource availability in other ways as well. As described in Chapter 3, moving a resource from point A to point B normally requires knowing:

- What resources (type and quantity) must be moved.

- When they must be moved (a time).

- Where they must be moved to (the destination).

- Where they must be moved from (the origin).

- How they must be moved (the transportation mode).

- The most expeditious route between the origin and the destination.

In many instances, we experience problems in immediately locating a resource's current origin. That is, we simply can't find what we're looking for, which in turn causes delays. In such instances, technology may prove a useful aid. For example, bar coding systems, location sensors, Global Positioning Systems, and an array of other wireless, data collection and transmitting devices, can help us more quickly locate a resource's current origin. Radio frequency identification (RFID) and tracking systems using radio transponders and interrogators can also help track the progress and route from a resource's origin to its final destination. By being able to quickly access such information, resources can be more rapidly located and moved from their origin to their destination. Such rapid movement increases the probability that a resource will be available at the right place and time, thereby maintaining schedule reliability.

Once again, by understanding the process and all required resources first, more informed decisions regarding technology design, acquisition, and implementation can be made. As illustrated by the C-17 Globemaster cargo plane example, a little process forethought can even eliminate the need for some required external resources altogether.

RESOURCE ACCESSIBILITY

As noted in Chapter 3, the ability to rapidly access resources is extremely important in any cycle time reduction initiative. Although a single delay associated with resource accessibility is normally quite small when compared to a single delay associated with resource availability, the high frequency of such delays quickly mounts up. As suggested in the previous chapters, the time devil is frequently associated with all of the insignificant things that we hardly ever think of. This is especially true when it comes to short, repetitive, high-frequency activities.

Technology fortunately has much to offer in terms of increasing resource accessibility. This observation is especially true when it comes to using computer-based information technologies to more quickly access job-related information. However, few companies have fully exploited this potential. Except for E-mailing and playing more sophisticated computer games, many people still use personal computers in much the same way that they always have.

In order to more rapidly access job-specific information, some companies are moving away from bulky and cumbersome paper-based systems. Instead, they are beginning to develop and use what some call Integrated Information Support Systems (IISS) or Electronic Performance Support Systems (EPSS). As defined and described by George and Emily Stevens[5], an EPSS is a "... computer-based tool designed to support access to job- or task-specific information by providing any of the following: training, reference information and expert advice, on demand as needed by the worker." An attractive feature of such systems is that they greatly increase information access speed.

Computer-based performance support systems have considerable applications for numerous industries, disciplines, and occupations.

This is especially true for mobile computer systems that can provide immediate support to people working outside of traditional office environments or who are constantly on the move. Such individuals may include service and maintenance technicians, sales people, mineral and petroleum exploration crews, assessors, inspectors, field representatives, nurses, paramedics, and emergency or disaster field teams. The one unifying theme concerning these individuals and groups is that they frequently require immediate access to large volumes of very different types of information. Yet, because of the sheer size associated with many paper-based systems, information access times are frequently quite slow. In some instances, associated volume prohibits even carrying the information into the field in the first place, completely preventing any type of access.

For example, to provide better and more rapid access to large amounts of maintenance-related information, one company developed an EPSS for its field maintenance crews. They call their system an Interactive Maintenance Support System or IMSS[6]. The system contains a number of features, including diagnostic flowcharts for trouble shooting, a step-by-step list of procedures for performing various maintenance activities, an illustrated parts breakdown of various components, operations manuals, and maintenance manuals.

All of this information is directly carried to a job site in a notebook computer. Whereas previously carrying an equivalent voluminous paper-based system was impractical, with a small notebook computer, it's now easily doable. The company found that maintenance personnel could not only access information much more rapidly, but they were also able to access more information which improved the quality, speed, and productivity of their work.

In this case, the process function of the technology is to decrease delays in searching for information by providing more immediate resource accessibility. Once again, by understanding the process function of a specific technology, we can gain greater benefit of that technology.

From a cycle time perspective it is important to ask how a given technology can eliminate, minimize, or combine various process steps. We also need to ask how a given technology may be used to minimize or even eliminate delays associated with unavailable or inaccessible resources.

Although it is important to understand the specifications of a particular technology, it is just as important to understand its function, especially as it relates to a work process. With greater process fore-thought, we can better optimize and utilize technology. In the following generic case study, reducing cycle time using technology will be explored.

CASE STUDY #3

Custom Life specializes in selling customized life insurance policies. The policies are specifically tailored to each individual client, both in terms of options and cost. Depending on various health-related risk factors—smoker vs. non-smoker, family history of heart disease, age, etc.—and selected options and payment plan (monthly, semi-annual, or annual), the cost and amount of coverage is adjusted accordingly. With such numerous options and contingencies, no two policies are ever exactly the same.

Custom Life also sells life insurance the old fashioned way. Its field agents, located throughout the nation, make numerous house calls, presenting the benefits and options of Custom Life policies to prospective buyers. If interested, potential customers are asked to fill out a lengthy application form which is then sent to the main office by the agent. At the main office, the application is evaluated and either accepted or refused. In some instances, a tentative acceptance is given contingent on successfully passing a medical examination.

If the application is accepted, a payment schedule is also determined. This information is then sent back to the field agent, who in turn contacts the prospective buyer with the information. Normally it takes about three to four weeks to receive acceptance approval and pricing information.

The president, who joined Custom Life only a few months before, decided to hold an information gathering meeting. She invited many of the field agents to the corporate office to hear their concerns and any suggested improvements that might better assist them in the field. Unfortunately, the new president wasn't prepared for all of the negative comments. Many of the field agents openly expressed their contempt and hostility for the way the company does business. It seemed that because of the lengthy delay before an insurance policy can actually be sold to a prospective customer, many customers change their minds or decide to go elsewhere. One agent said, "Because we're so slow, hot customers quickly turn into cold ones and we lose the sale. Our response time in meeting customer needs is absolutely dismal."

The president, deeply concerned by these remarks, asked the field agents what they would like instead of the current system. In an almost unanimous chorus, they replied, "To close the deal immediately." The president thanked the field agents for their frankness and promised to look into the matter the very next day.

The next day, she met with the manager who oversees application approvals and costing. The president expressed her concerns and findings, noting the need to dramatically reduce customer response times. The Approval & Costing manager, however, scoffed at the agents' rumblings, noting that they have to have "at least something to complain about." He further described how his department's application and costing process was fully computerized and automated two years ago. What more can he do, he argued, and besides, his people are working as fast as they can. If the new president wants faster service, she needs to give the manager more people. The president perceived that she was getting nowhere with the discussion and thanked the manager for his time. Realizing that there is little internal support for changing anything in the Approval and Costing department, she decided to bring in an outside consultant.

A week later, the president briefed the consultant on her concerns, as well as related to him the ideal system from the field agent's perspective. Together, they outlined a plan of action. The consultant first mapped out the current process using the Seven-Step PI Method and collected all related process times. After fully understanding the current process, he then determined if it was feasible to give the field agents what they want.

The consultant began observing and mapping the approval and costing process. He also collected all related time data. The manager of the affected department, however, was quite upset with the intrusion. He offered only minimal support, along with some very open hostility.

The consultant determined that the approval and costing process began by receiving a customer application form from a field agent. After a delay of a few days, while the form sat idly in an "in" basket, the process continued as follows:

1. A clerk enters all of the information from the paper form into a computer, where it becomes the exact same "electronic" form.

2. The form is sent to an evaluator via the company's computer network. This person determines the applicant's acceptability and associated risk factors. Seventy-two percent of the time the application is accepted, 22 percent of the time a medical examination is required, and 6 percent of the time the application is rejected outright.

3. The form is then electronically mailed to a supervisor who reviews the acceptance determination and either concurs with it or sends it back for any needed changes.

4. If approved, the form is sent electronically to someone else who calculates a payment schedule. If a medical examination is required, the field agent is notified by phone and processing of the application is temporarily halted.

5. After a payment schedule has been calculated, the electronic form is sent to yet another supervisor who reviews the payment schedule and either concurs or returns it for necessary changes.

6. At this stage, the application has been accepted and a payment schedule has been determined. The form is then electronically mailed to a senior reviewer, who goes over the completed package. Once this person is satisfied (and it's only *one* person), the agent in the field is sent the information by way of first-class postage.

Unfortunately, this description doesn't capture all of the lengthy delays resulting from the electronic form waiting in an electronic queue or computer "in" basket. Most of these delays are associated with waiting for review and approval signatures.

The consultant mapped out the entire process and collected all related time data. The completed process analysis worksheet is illustrated in Figure 4.1. He then created a data summary chart, a percent cycle-time bar graph, and a value-added/non-value-added pie chart. These displays are illustrated in Figure 4.2.

As depicted in Figure 4.2, true value-added time is less than 1 percent. All other time is associated with lengthy delays and multiple reviews. Intrigued by the remark that the process was "computerized

#	Step Description	Flow	Time (Minutes)	Resources	Notes
1	Application sits in "in" basket	D	960		
2	Inputed into computer	®	20	1	
3	Electronically mailed	⇨	1		
4	Waits in computer queue	D	180		
5	Acceptability assessed	O	20	1	
6	Electronically mailed	⇨	1		
7	Waits in computer queue	D	180		
8	Supervisor review	□	10	1	
9	Electronically mailed	⇨	1		
10	Waits in computer queue	D	180		
11	Payment determined	O	20	1	
12	Electronically mailed	⇨	1		
13	Waits in computer queue	D	180		
14	Supervisor review	□	5	1	
15	Electronically mailed	⇨	1		
16	Waits in computer queue	D	240		
17	Final review and approval	□	5	1	
18	Mailed to field agent	⇨	1440		

FIGURE 4.1. Process analysis worksheet for insurance application process.

and automated two years ago," the consultant researched the old process. What he quickly discovered was that the new process simply represents a digitized version of the old one. Nothing really changed, nor was anything actually automated. Essentially, a paper medium was replaced by a digital one with no accompanying fundamental process design changes. Computer queues simply replaced paper "in" baskets and the number of reviews and authorizations actually increased by one. About the only thing that decreased was internal office transportation times.

Step Type	# of Steps	Minutes
Operation	2	40
Transportation	6	1445
Delay	6	1920
Inspection	3	20
Storage		
Rework	1	20
Total	18	3590

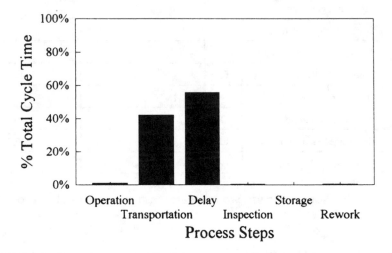

FIGURE 4.2. Data summaries for insurance application process.

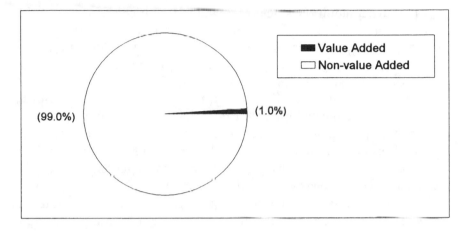

FIGURE 4.2. (*continued*).

The consultant further investigated what was involved in determining insurability (acceptability) and price scheduling. It turns out that a series of "if—then" decision trees are used. For example, *If client smokes greater than two packs of cigarettes a day and has a family history of heart problems and is 50 years of age, then a medical examination is required*. These various "if—then" rules are kept in thick manuals at each worker's desk. Supervisor reviews consist simply of ensuring that the proper decision tree branches are selected and correctly followed.

Relating his findings to the president of Custom Life, the consultant proposed a new process. He suggested that each field agent, who would now be called a case manager, be equipped with a notebook computer that contains a life insurance application software program with an embedded decision support system. The decision support system contains the company's "if—then" rules. Instead of having perspective customers fill out a lengthy application form, the agent would instead ask various questions and input this data directly into the computer. Depending on the answer received, the program would automatically branch along a different pathway to another question. For example, if the potential customer has always been a non-smoker, the program would bypass numerous smoking-related questions.

Once acceptability has been determined, a price schedule would be immediately calculated. If the perspective buyer accepts the policy, the completed application would be electronically transferred via modem to the main office, where it would be uploaded into the records and accounts payable computer system. Initial payment and all actual acceptance signatures would follow in the mail. As an added bonus, the consultant suggested giving a first-year discount to potential customers who purchase the policy that same day. With the newly redesigned process, cycle times would be reduced from three or four weeks to only an hour or two. Also, the case manager is now directly responsible for completing all of the steps in the application approval and costing process. The redesigned process has essentially created a one-stop and one-person shop; the case manager becoming that one-person and the notebook computer creating the one-stop shop.

The president liked the conceptual redesign and presented it to a group of field agents. They endorsed the proposed process change enthusiastically and offered their complete assistance. The president then contacted a software developer who specializes in writing such programs. To the president's surprise, the software developer told her that the application is actually very straightforward and easy to develop. This is mainly because of the straightforward logic of the rule structures used by the company. In addition, if price rates or insurability risk factors should change, the program can be easily modified and transferred to all field agents via a modem. Although there would be some upfront costs in software development, computer hardware purchase, and initial training, these costs would hopefully quickly be offset by increased sales.

The president met next with the manager of the affected department. Not surprisingly, he opposed the proposed process redesign adamantly, citing many reasons why it would not work. He also angrily pointed out that she would essentially be wiping out his entire department. The president countered that although it is true that his department would be significantly reduced, it could assume a different supporting role and oversee the new software's development, implementation, and continued use. Additionally, anyone not needed in his department would be transferred within the company, with no resultant job loss. This, the manager defiantly stated, was still completely unsatisfactory. It's his department and he should be able to run it as he sees fit. The president ended the meeting and asked him to think over the proposal and get back to her the next day.

At the next meeting the affected manager was still unwilling to change. The president determined that any continued persuasion was useless and that the needs of the company must take precedent over the individual wishes of a single manager. In the end, she ordered the redesigned process implemented. She disbanded the opposing manager's department completely and assigned a new manager and group to oversee the software development effort and provide ongoing support. She transferred some personnel in the old department to other positions in the company. Unfortunately, others in the department, including the affected manager, decided to leave Custom Life.

The cycle time reduction effort turned out to be a resounding success for the company, with sales increasing significantly. Case managers are now able to close many sales at the time they make their initial presentation. Whereas before the company simply replaced a bad paper-based process with a bad computer-based process, this time they fundamentally changed the process to leverage the power of an existing technology. This fundamental change was made possible by the careful selection and application of a specific technology.

SUMMARY

Technology, especially computer-based information and communications technologies, can be a useful ally in reducing process cycle times. However, technology should never be viewed as a magical panacea, capable of solving all cycle time-related problems. Instead, considerable process forethought must be given to its use and specific application. For example, simply computerizing a bad paper-based process usually results in having a bad computer-based process, with little or no reduction in cycle time.

In applying technology, it is always important to understand the process first, and then determine how a specific technology may serve a specific process function. As noted, technology can be used to reduce cycle times in a number of ways. These include the following:

• Eliminating various steps from a process.

- Minimizing the time duration of associated process steps.

- Combining two or more process steps.

- Improving resource availability.

- Improving resource accessibility.

When used intelligently and with a specific process function in mind, technology can greatly reduce cycle times.

5 —— CONTINUOUS FLOW

The first three basic principles of cycle time reduction involve eliminating process waste, providing the right resources at the right place and time, and using technology to improve process flow. In this chapter, we'll explore the fourth basic principle of cycle time reduction—creating continuous flow.

In continuous flow, as noted in Chapter 1, products, materials, information, goods, people, and just about everything else, move continuously, stopping only when value is directly being added. In an idealized continuous process flow, there are no delays. Only short stops that directly add value to a customer or object. Although the concept of continuous flow originated in the manufacturing sector, it is applicable to any business environment or industry. One hospital, for example, uses the term "patient flow" to represent continuous flow.

To experience the concept of continuous flow, let's go on an imaginary business trip. Our trip requires us to fly non stop from Dallas to Chicago. What would continuous process flow be like? First, as we arrive at the Dallas airport in our own car, we drive directly to an open parking space. No unnecessary delays caused by searching for an empty space are encountered. Then we walk directly to the airline ticket counter where there are no waiting lines. There our plane ticket is quickly processed and our baggage is checked. Then we proceed directly to our boarding gate and immediately board the plane. Once safely seated, the plane instantly pushes back from the gate. It then taxies out onto the runway and takes off without delay. As we approach Chicago, we are immediately cleared for landing. Once on the ground, our plane proceeds directly to its assigned gate. As soon as the plane is safely parked, we immediately get up from our seat and proceed to the baggage claim area without any delays. As we arrive at the baggage claim area, our bags are waiting for us. We grab our bags (hardly breaking stride) and proceed out the door to a waiting rental car van. As the van takes us to the car rental parking lot, our paperwork is processed enroute. Once at our rental car, we load our baggage into the trunk and immediately drive out of the Chicago airport. That's continuous flow. Reading this description, most of us who fly a great deal would probably happily settle for even "semi-continuous flow."

As illustrated in the process flow diagram in Figure 5.1, most processes, such as flying from Dallas to Chicago, involve numerous delays. In an idealized continuous flow situation, however, these delays are eliminated and theoretical cycle time is achieved. The process is now composed basically of only operation and transportation steps. This idealized process flow condition is illustrated in Figure 5.2. Compare the difference between the two figures. If Figure 5.1 and 5.2 represent the same process, it's obvious which one will have the shorter cycle times. This is why the concept of continuous flow is so important. Continuous flow equals speed.

FIGURE 5.1. A typical process flow containing numerous delays.

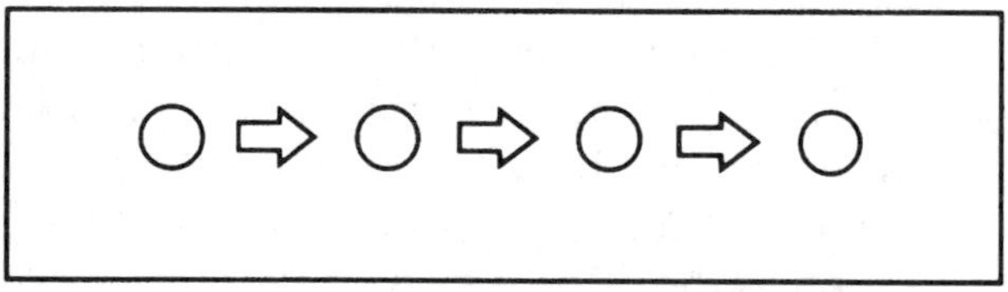

O ⇨ O ⇨ O ⇨ O

FIGURE 5.2. The same process as in Figure 5.1, but without all of the associated delays.

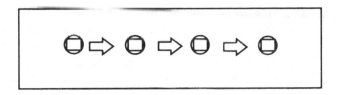

FIGURE 5.3. The same process as in Figure 5.2, but with combined operation/inspection steps.

In addition, should our process require certain inspections to be performed, they're combined with operation steps, illustrated in Figure 5.3. Once again, no delays are present in Figure 5.3 and continuous flow is maintained.

Although the concept of continuous work flow may sound impossible to achieve, the simple fact that a company attempts such a quest can lead to significant reductions in cycle time. When attempting to achieve continuous flow, however, companies must look at an entire process from beginning to end. This assures that all process steps and activities become interdependent elements of a larger, single process, seamlessly connected. It does little good to attempt to create continuous flow in the manufacturing department, only to have finished goods sit for long periods of time in a distribution warehouse. Instead, we must view manufacturing and distribution as one combined process. This process includes making and getting goods to customers as quickly as possible. In continuous flow then, we must look at the entire value delivery system from its very beginning to its final end.

Many things can prevent or impede continuous process flow including unnecessary and time-consuming delays and other non-value-adding process steps. It also includes not having the right resources at the right place and time. Continuous flow also can be interrupted by the misapplication of technology. In the following sections, we'll explore three other elements that can affect continuous flow. These three elements are:

- Chokepoints. Chokepoints, also referred to as process bottlenecks, represent mega-delays. Chokepoints can significantly interrupt process flow and cause extensive backlogs.

- Capacity Limitations. In some instances, work volume exceeds the capacity limitations of both human and machine resources. Under such conditions delays occur, continuous flow is interrupted, and cycle times are extended. In many instances, the leveling or moderating of work volume can improve continuous flow.

- Process layout. A poorly designed process or physical work layout can easily interrupt process flow and unnecessarily lengthen cycle times.

In the following section, the adverse effect of process chokepoints will be discussed.

CHOKEPOINTS

We can think of a process as being analogous to a river. Let's imagine that we want to float logs from the upstream portion of the river downstream as quickly as possible. Our process begins with rolling a log into the upstream portion of the river one at a time and ends with taking each log out of the river downstream. Ideally, we want our logs to float continuously downriver without any unnecessary delays or interruptions.

Yet, as the logs journey downriver, they sometimes get stuck at certain chokepoints scattered along the river. At such points they begin to bunch up and, as a result, logjams are created. Such logjams interrupt process flow. In Figure 5.4, we can illustrate such chokepoints by using a delay symbol. If we are to achieve continuous flow

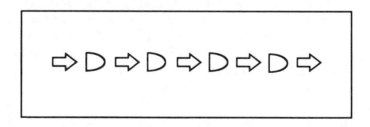

FIGURE 5.4. A transportation sequence interrupted by numerous delays. In many instances, such delays can represent major process chokepoints.

with our logs, we must identify where these major chokepoints occur. Then we must eliminate them from our process (the river).

This same concept of chokepoints and their identification and elimination can be applied to any process. When we initially examine a work process, we frequently find a few mega-delays that represent major chokepoints and seriously affect overall process flow. If we do nothing more than simply identify and eliminate these major delays, we can almost always significantly reduce cycle time.

For example, one company mapped one of its major processes using the Seven-Step PI Method. The company found that the process contained 150 individual process steps, of which 40 were identified as delay steps. These 40 delay steps accounted for 90 percent of total cycle time. This percentage contribution is graphically depicted in Figure 5.5. Yet, of the 40 identified delay steps, three of them accounted for 40 percent of the total cycle time associated with only delays. That is, of the total cycle time, 36 percent was associated with just three delay steps. If these three delay steps can be eliminated or greatly minimized, a very significant reduction in cycle time can be instantly achieved.

Although many companies know that they have a bad process creating significant delays and associated backlogs, they may have lit-

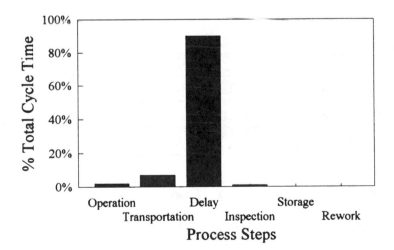

FIGURE 5.5. A percent total cycle time bar graph. Note the significant associated total delay time.

...ea exactly where such delays are located. Or even worse, they mistakenly think they know where such problems are located. One company, for example, was convinced that its procurement department was responsible for creating significant work backlogs. Yet when the company systematically observed and mapped the process, they found something quite different. The chokepoint was actually upstream from procurement, residing in another department altogether. Ironically, the department actually creating the chokepoint had been complaining the most about procurement.

If companies can only take the time to systematically map and quantify their processes, such chokepoints become obvious. As illustrated in the process analysis worksheet displayed in Figure 5.6, chokepoints are easily identifiable, usually sticking out like a red herring. For example, the circled delay step in Figure 5.6 accounts for a disproportionate amount of cycle time. It represents a major process chokepoint.

A few major chokepoints in a process then can cause major delays. Commonly, these few delays account for a significantly disproportionate amount of total cycle time. If we are to significantly reduce cycle time and create continuous flow, it is critical to identify these major process chokepoints. We must either eliminate or significantly minimize them.

#	Step Description	Flow	Time (Min)	Resources	Notes
1	Component A assembled	◯	15	1	
2	Transferred on conveyor	⇨	5		
3	Component A & B assembled	◯	20	1	
4	Transferred on conveyor	⇨	5		
5	Waiting for quality inspection	▷	(300)		
6	Assembly inspected	☐	10	1	

FIGURE 5.6. Chokepoints, which represent significant delays, are usually quite obvious in any process analysis worksheet.

As will be explored in the next section, process chokepoints are sometimes caused by exceeding the capacity limitations of both human and machine resources. Before continuing, however, it is important to make one additional comment about process chokepoints. Some suggest that we simply throw out a bad process and start over from scratch. Often, however, the identification and elimination of a few major chokepoints in a process can bring about the same radical effect. Before being so quick to eliminate a bad process, it's important to understand why it's bad. Without such knowledge, we are likely to recreate the same problem in our "reengineered" version.

CAPACITY LIMITATIONS

Sometimes, chokepoints in a process are caused by exceeding the capacity limitation of key resources. These resources can be either human or machine. *Capacity* is defined as the potential output over some allotted time period. For example, a photocopier machine has a capacity rating of so many pages per minute, or a data entry clerk can input into a computer only so much information per hour. These resource capacity limitations are important to understand, both in terms of cycle time reduction as well as potential productivity levels.

Commonly, however, such capacity ratings represent hypothetical or ideal capacities. To determine actual or real working capacities, we must normally multiply hypothetical capacity ratings by *availability*. Availability refers to the percentage of time that a resource is actually available for use.

For example, a photocopier machine must be periodically stopped to remove jammed paper, reload paper, add toner, or perform preventive maintenance services. During these times, the machine is not available for use. Similarly, a data entry clerk during the course of a day takes breaks, attends meetings, as well as does other tasks. Also during the course of a month, the clerk may be sick, or take vacation time. Like the photocopier machine, during these off times, the clerk is not available for use. That is, the data entry clerk can't enter data.

To determine actual capacity, hypothetical capacity must be multiplied by resource availability, as follows:

Actual Capacity = Hypothetical Capacity
× Resource Availability

In determining actual capacity, we commonly use 0.8 for an availability figure. That is, 80 percent of the time, a resource is available for use. This 0.8 availability figure may vary significantly, however. It's always best to actually measure availability whenever possible. One company, for example, found that worker availability was only 20 percent when actually measured.

Using this 0.8 availability figure and assuming a theoretical capacity of 50 entries per hour for a data entry clerk, we can easily calculate actual capacity. Actual capacity equals 50 × 0.8 or 40 entries per hour. A daily average then is 320 entries per 8-hour work day (8 × 40). Compare this 320 entry figure to a hypothetical capacity of 400 entries per day.

Let's further assume that the data entry department receives on average 1,100 forms to enter per day. It also has only three data entry clerks. If actual capacity is 320 entries per day, then daily departmental capacity is 320 × 3 (number of clerks) or 960 entries per day. In this instance, actual capacity is exceeded by 140 forms per day (1100 – 960). A resultant backlog will accrue at the rate of 140 forms per day. In terms of cycle time and continuous flow, a significant delay or process chokepoint has been created. The chokepoint is caused by exceeding the resource capacity of the three data entry clerks.

The following two examples illustrate how capacity-related chokepoints can adversely impede continuous flow and lengthen cycle time. In the first example, a company has just switched from a paper-based procurement process to a computer-based one. The move was intended to greatly reduce process cycle times. It was also intended to eliminate a large and growing backlog. This reduction in backlog is extremely important since the procurement department processes thousands of requisition orders per month. Yet, after six months of using the new computer-based system, overall cycle times have changed very little, and, even more disturbing, the same backlog rate is accruing.

Confused and frustrated, the company's general manager charged a team with fixing the problem. The team held a number of brainstorming sessions. From such sessions they created a long list of ideas about what's wrong with the new system. Although such meetings were well facilitated and organized, they represented little more than personal-opinion sessions and little progress was made. Finally realizing that something different must be done, the team decided to systematically map the process and collect quantitative data, using the Seven-Step PI Method. The team became one with the procurement process and traveled with a requisition form throughout the process.

The team initially identified a number of short delays. None, however, accounted for the massive backlog. Near the end of the process-mapping exercise, the team discovered a major chokepoint. Years ago, when the procurement process was originally set up, all requisitions went through one person for final review and approval. Ironically, this final single-person verification step has never been changed. It was also incorporated into the new computer-based process design with little forethought as to its adverse effects.

The person currently doing this final verification step is senior in the department. She is continuously bragging about how hard she works and how productive she is. The process mapping team discovered that indeed she is very hard working and productive. She verifies, on average, 80 procurement requisitions per day. Yet, when the team determined her daily work volume, they found that an average of 140 requisitions are being sent to her each day. In essence, the capacity of this one human resource is being exceeded by 60 procurement requisitions per day ($140 - 80 = 60$). The team further determined that this one single delay accounts for 65 percent of all related process delay times.

Armed with this knowledge, the team prepared to make a decision on how to resolve the problem. The team realized that one alternative is to completely eliminate the final verification step. This would remove the chokepoint altogether. Another alternative is to add one additional human resource to the final verification step. This would allow adequate resource capacity, since two people can verify 160 requisitions per day ($80 \times 2 = 160$). This in turn would restore continuous flow through this particular process step. The two ideas were presented to management, who evaluated the real value-adding worth of this step. They decided to simply eliminate the step altogether. Something, according to one manager, that should have been done years ago.

In another example, a small manufacturing company has just started producing a new mechanical accessory. Surprisingly, the response to the new product has been outstanding. Delighted by the product's reception, management orders that production levels be doubled and production cycle times slashed. Unfortunately, such demands can't be met. This is especially true in two of the departments responsible for producing many of the individual components that go into the product's final assembly.

The rather autocratic president of the company thinks he knows why these two particular departments can't meet his demands. Wage issues have arisen during the company's overnight success and the president is convinced that the inability to increase productivity and reduce cycle time is simply a ploy by the workforce to increase wages.

One member of senior management, however, is not convinced that this is necessarily true. He begins to question why only two of the departments are experiencing problems. The other three departments involved in the production and assembly process have successfully cut cycle times and increased productivity. The senior manager requests that the process flow in the two problem departments be mapped and time data collected. As these two departments use a number of machines in their production process, he also requests that actual capacities for these machines be determined as well.

The collected data is most informative. Given the current number and capacity of machines in the two departments, it is simply impossible to achieve the demanded increases in productivity and associated decreases in cycle time. There is insufficient capacity for two of the machines in one department and for one of the machines in the other department. The senior manager realizes that these two departments must either begin double shifting or purchase three new additional machines.

Calculations indicate that it is cheaper to buy three new machines than to go to the expense of adding a second shift. In the redesigned process, parts now diverge to two identical machines, later converging to continue their flow in a linear fashion. This redesigned process flow is illustrated graphically in Figure 5.7.

The senior manager presents his findings to the president of the company. The president, once presented with the collected data, grudgingly accepts the senior manager's recommendation. However, he is still not completely convinced that he doesn't have a worker problem on his hands.

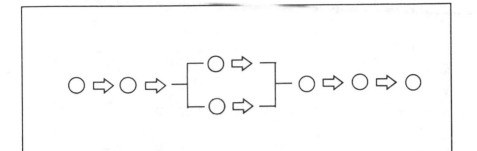

FIGURE 5.7. A redesigned process that diverges to accommodate increased capacity.

The systematic identification and elimination of chokepoints in a process, then, is critical to significantly reducing cycle times and creating continuous flow. In some instances, such chokepoints are caused by exceeding capacity limitations of both human and equipment resources. Understanding required throughput volumes and determining matching resource capacities is crucial to preventing process chokepoints.

It's also important when attempting to create continuous flow to differentiate between real capacity limitations and capacity surges. In many instances, perceived capacity limitations are actually only temporary surges that occur over brief periods of time. Sometimes, work leveling can help moderate such surges.

In Figure 5.8, work volume over an eight-hour period is plotted for a particular machine. A horizontal dashed line shows the capacity limit per hour for the machine. The graphed data indicate that for an eight-hour period, total machine capacity is not exceeded. Continuous flow is, at least, theoretically possible. However, at certain times of the day, the capacity of the machine is exceeded. This condition is indicated in Figure 5.8 by work volume exceeding hourly machine capacity. As a result of these work surges, temporary delays occur and small backlogs begin accruing. These backlogs are eliminated in subsequent hours when machine capacity is under utilized.

Sometimes such work surges are unavoidable and must be accepted as part of doing business. For example, customer traffic at a small downtown restaurant always surges at lunchtime. At such

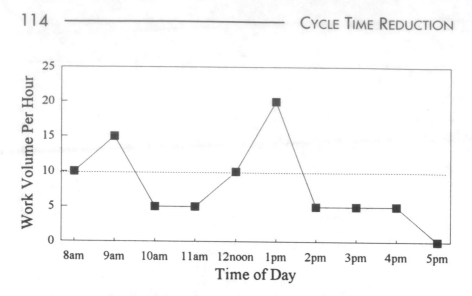

FIGURE 5.8. A line graph depicting work volume per hour. Horizontal dashed line indicates volume capacity per hour.

times, the capacity limits of the restaurant (available tables, waitresses, cooks) may be exceeded and customer delays occur. At other times of the day, however, there is abundant capacity. In such instances, it simply may not be economically feasible to provide adequate resources (including space and staff) to meet periodic excesses of capacity during only a short lunch period.

In other instances, capacity surges may be avoided or significantly minimized through work leveling. Work leveling refers to the practice of controlling work volume so that process flow is optimized. Referring back to the graph in Figure 5.8, capacity surges can be prevented if work volume can be moderated to match existing machine capacity. The results of this work leveling or moderation effort is illustrated in Figure 5.9; hourly machine capacities are no longer exceeded.

The following example illustrates how the concept of work leveling may be applied in preventing sporadic interruptions in continuous work flow. An environmental company is contracted to demolish a highly contaminated plant complex. The plant complex was previously used in the manufacturing of very hazardous and toxic materials. During the demolition process, it is very important to continuously sample levels of contamination. This sampling information

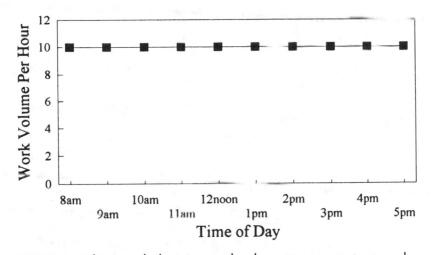

FIGURE 5.9. A line graph depicting work volume at a constant rate and equal to volume capacity per hour.

determines the specific classification and subsequent storage of the generated waste, and also determines the sequencing of the various demolition activities and the required mixing and packaging of the various waste materials.

The company ideally would like real-time sampling feedback. This would create a continuous process flow from waste sampling to waste analysis and characterization, to actual demolition and waste packaging. However, the company will accept a one-hour turn-around time by the onsite analytical laboratory. Unfortunately, this is not being accomplished. Numerous complaints are being voiced by demolition supervisors who require analytical information to plan their demolition sequence and waste packaging methods.

The general manager of the company meets with the head of the analytical laboratory and voices his concern and displeasure with the lab's current performance. He wants sample process cycle times significantly reduced and more information made available to his demolition supervisors. The head of the lab, however, argues that they already have a very efficient process in place. If the general manager wants faster turnaround times, he needs to supply the lab with additional analytical equipment and personnel to run the equipment. The general manager is not convinced that this is the real problem. He first wants to assure himself that they have a good process in place and that they aren't needlessly interrupting process flow.

The process is mapped in some detail using the Seven-Step PI Method. The mapped process begins with initially taking a sample at the demolition site and ends with completing the analysis in the laboratory and sending the results to the demolition supervisors. Also, the average number of samples collected each day are compared to the actual capacity of the laboratory. It's determined that an average of 90 samples are collected for laboratory analysis each day. The laboratory, however, has an actual capacity limitation of 15 samples per hour. This translates into 120 samples for an eight hour period. To everyone's surprise, the lab actually has an excess capacity of some 30 samples. So what is causing the problem?

Backlog sample volumes for each hour of the day are tracked in the lab for a one week period. An average of these daily backlogs-per-hour measurement is graphically illustrated in Figure 5.10. Also indicated by the horizontal dashed line in Figure 5.10 is the 15 sample per hour actual capacity of the laboratory.

As shown in Figure 5.10, two volume surges are experienced by the analytical laboratory each day. A smaller one at noon, which dumps, on average, 30 samples into the analysis stream, and a much

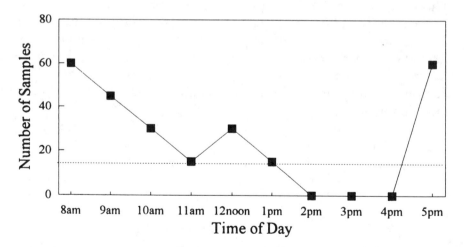

FIGURE 5.10. A line graph depicting work volume per hour. Horizontal dashed line indicates volume capacity per hour.

larger one at 5:00 p.m., which dumps 60 samples into the lab system. This late night dumping creates an immediate backlog of 60 samples the next morning. Comparing this information with the detailed process analysis worksheet that was also generated, the source of the problem is quickly identified.

The analytical laboratory is located some distance from the actual demolition site. The sampling crew, who work for the demolition supervisors, normally drop their samples off at the laboratory at night on their way home. This way they can always leave a bit early. Some crew members also drop samples off at the lab just before lunch time. This practice gives them a head start to the cafeteria each day. Each time they drop samples off at the lab, they also pick up any analytical results which is later delivered to demolition supervisors. Unfortunately, this twice-a-day drop off surges the capacity of the analytical laboratory.

When finally understanding the problem, the general manager realizes that the company has committed a common mistake. It has failed to look at the continuous flow of the whole sampling and analytical process from beginning to end. Instead, the company has designed only parts of the process, failing to connect those parts at crucial process junctures. By doing so, the company has created unnecessary interruptions and delays in overall process flow.

Everyone realizes that the analytical laboratory has adequate throughput capacity. What is required, however, is that sample volume be leveled or moderated to match laboratory processing capacity. An employee is assigned to be a sample runner. His job is to collect samples from the sampling crew and transport them to the laboratory each hour. He then returns current analysis results to the demolition supervisors.

The company is amazed and rather embarrassed that they have neglected such a simple thing. They realize that if cycle times are to be significantly reduced and continuous process flow attained, they must design efficient processes from beginning to end. Narrow-sighted functional or departmental approaches to process design can easily create unnecessary chokepoints and capacity surges at critical process junctures.

The above example illustrates the use of work leveling to prevent capacity surges. Work volume surges can adversely affect process cycle times and disrupt continuous process flow. Also illustrated in this example, is the negative effect that a physical layout of a process can potentially have on continuous flow. This topic will be covered in the next section.

PROCESS LAYOUT

The actual physical layout of a work process can also impede continuous work flow. In many instances, a poor physical layout can cause numerous delays and process flow interruptions. By carefully considering various process layout options, such interruptions can sometimes be significantly minimized and in many instances, eliminated altogether.

As noted earlier, the concept of continuous flow had its origins in the manufacturing sector. Traditionally, manufacturing companies grouped various machines by function. That is, all drill presses were placed in one area and all metal lathes in another. They also created different "shops." These shops included a separate carpenter shop, metal shop, paint shop, and pipefitting shop. When manufacturing a product then, parts and components would travel from one functional machine grouping to another, as well as from shop to shop. This concept is illustrated in Figure 5.11.

As illustrated in Figure 5.11, this physical layout created a number of inefficiencies. For example, it required numerous transportation steps, sometimes of considerable distances, among the various functional machine groupings and shops. It also required that materials and semi-finished parts had to travel back and forth among the same buildings or same functional machine groups multiple times. Both instances increased cycle time.

Additionally, the coordination required by all of these transportation moves frequently caused time-consuming delays, which severely interrupted process flow. In some instances, a simple 15 minute job actually took three days when all of the associated transportation and delay times were included.

The manufacturing industry realized that functionally grouping machines, in many instances, was inefficient. To improve this situation, they began to examine the actual process flow of making something. For example, the actual flow of a process may require that material stock go first to some type of stamping machine. The rough

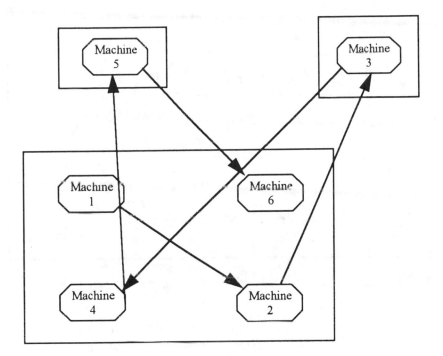

FIGURE 5.11. A very inefficient physical layout causing lengthy transportation distances and associated delays.

part is then turned next on a metal lathe and then sent to a drill press. Next it goes to another machine for polishing and so on. As noted, these various machines were traditionally scattered throughout a large work area or even housed in separate buildings.

People began to realize that in many instances it would make much more sense to have the machines grouped according to process flow. That is, whenever possible, to group a stamping machine next to a metal lathe, the metal lathe next to a drill press, etc. Such process groupings would greatly minimize transportation distances and times associated with traveling among the various machines. It would also eliminate delays associated with having to move parts and components among various functional machine groupings or buildings.

Based on this idea, the manufacturing industry began to arrange and group machines differently. Such practices, commonly called cellular manufacturing in the United States and production islands in

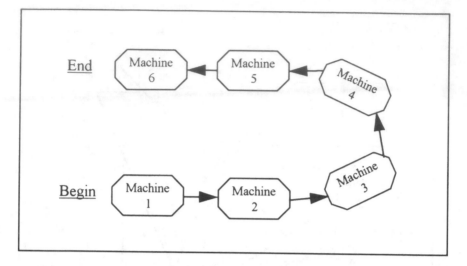

FIGURE 5.12. A U-shaped, cellular layout. Compare with Figure 5.11.

Europe, grouped machines according to process flow. In many in-stances, this allowed for the near continuous flow of parts through a manufacturing process. Figure 5.12 depicts this process approach to work layout. Compare the differences between Figures 5.11 and 5.12. A more-or-less continuous flow has been achieved in Figure 5.12. Not graphically captured in Figure 5.12, however, are the nu-merous delays that have also been eliminated by the more efficient layout.

In some instances, physical layouts are determined more by de-partmental politics than by good process reasoning. One company, for example, had a simple two-step operation to process some of its materials. However, between these two operational steps, a short test was required. Unfortunately, the specific equipment required to per-form the simple test was housed in another building. So every time the first part of the operation was completed, the initially processed material had to be:

1. Packaged for shipping.

2. Moved to a loading dock.

3. Transported across the plantsite to the testing shop.

4. Unloaded.

5. Unpackaged.

6. Tested (which took about five minutes).

7. Repackaged.

8. Placed on the testing shop's loading dock.

9. Retransported across the plantsite.

10. Unloaded.

11. Unpackaged.

12. Made ready for the next operation step.

The reason for such foolish inefficiencies was that the testing manager insisted that all of his test equipment be kept at one central location. In this case, however, the needed test equipment was used only for this particular process. Why it couldn't be placed directly at the site of the operation was simply controlled by one manger's need for control. This personal need created a completely unnecessary interruption in process flow and unwarranted process-related costs.

It is important when attempting to improve continuous work flow to always optimize the physical layout of any process. By doing so, many unnecessary interruptions that impede process flow can be either eliminated or significantly minimized.

By identifying and eliminating process chokepoints, determining capacity limitations, leveling or moderating work volumes, and improving process layouts, we can greatly improve the continuous flow of any work process. The following generic case study illustrates the application of some of these improvement suggestions, especially as they relate to increasing continuous work flow by improving the physical layout of a process.

Case Study #4

A successful businessman in a large city has just been presented an opportunity to purchase a small printing and copying company. The company caters to mid-size printing jobs, normally in the hundreds to thousands copy range. The company has been quite successful, frequently having to turn away new business. The company has also successfully expanded its operations over the past two years. It now owns four separate stores scattered throughout the city. The reason for the sale is that the current owner has recently experienced serious health problems. He has been advised by his doctor to sell the company and retire to a warmer and drier climate.

The interested businessman occasionally purchases small to mid-size companies like this printing company. To make such investments, however, he has developed some very stringent screening criteria including:

- The company must be small to mid-size and be in some type of service business.

- It must do high-volume, high-frequency work with relatively short turnaround times.

- The initial sale price must represent a high to moderate long-term value.

- The company must have a high potential for increased profitability with only minimal capital investment. That is, the businessman does not want to increase profitability through large, additional capital expenditures.

To further help in his selection process, he has developed a simple decision matrix, illustrated in Table 5.1. The two determining factors in the matrix are increased potential profitability and value of sale. Only those companies that fall in the high/high or high/medium sectors are considered for purchase. Those companies following in lower sectors are rejected outright.

The businessman tours the four stores and is quite impressed with what he sees. All four stores are setup almost identically, are spotlessly clean, and appear to be well organized. The various machines used in the printing and copying processes, which represent six distinct work stations, are laid out with almost military precision, each facing in the exact same direction. Storage cabinets, placed some distance from the machines, appear to be well stocked and organized. Employees also seem to work very hard, scurrying among

TABLE 5.1. DECISION MATRIX

		Increased Potential Profitability		
		Low	**Medium**	**High**
	High			
Value of Sale	**Medium**			
	Low			

the various work stations burdened with orders in process. While at two of the stores, he observes customer orders that have to be turned away because they can not be processed quickly enough.

When he asks employees what is needed to increase productivity and cut turnaround times (cycle time), the answer is always the same, "more machines." But buying more machines represents a large capital investment, something the prospective buyer is unwilling to do.

The businessman is convinced that the selling price is a good buy and represents high market value. Unfortunately, he sees little potential for increasing profitability unless he makes some very sizable capital investments in purchasing additional equipment. However, he has learned in the past that what appears to be a very efficient and productive process may actually have significant room for improvement. He contacts a consultant who specializes in cycle time reduction and productivity improvement to assess the company's potential for improvement. Specifically, the businessman wants to know if cycle times can be reduced and productivity increased without purchasing additional machines.

The consultant visits each of the four stores. He observes the process and quickly creates a rough process analysis worksheet on which he collects all associated time data, as well as physical distances walked by employees in going from one machine to another. He also draws a map of the work stations and storage cabinets on his notebook computer. This initial work station layout is illustrated in Figure 5.13. He then asks for copies of the last 500 work orders from two of the stores.

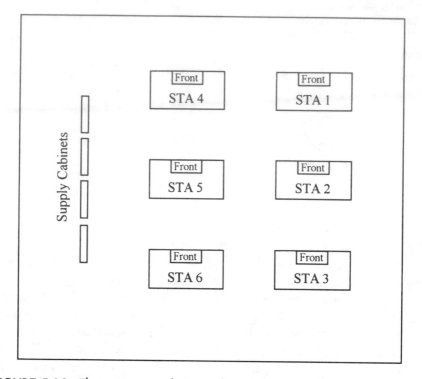

FIGURE 5.13. The existing work station layout.

Examining the work orders, the consultant discovers that the company offers various printing services, such as one- or two-sided printing, three-hole punching, binding, stapling, etc. He then correlates each of these services with a specific work station and assigns a work station number (previously identified in Figure 5.13). He next calculates the various flow paths and their frequencies from work station to work station, which are determined by customer order requests. For example, one flow path may be two-sided copying and three-hole punching. From this analysis, he discovers that there are four basic flow paths. He records these, along with their percentage of occurrence, as the following:

- From work station #1 to #6, 45% of the time.
- From work station #4 to #6, 30% of the time.

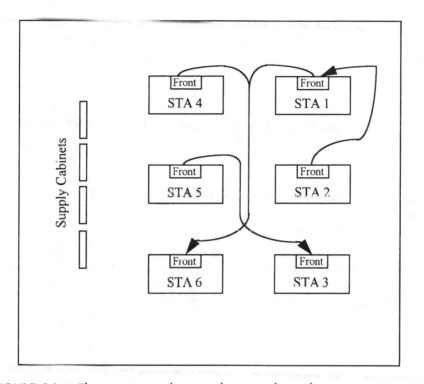

FIGURE 5.14. The existing work station layout with employee transportation routes among the various work stations.

- From work station #2 to #1 to #6, 15% of the time.
- From work station #5 to #3, 10% of the time.

He next maps these flow paths on his initial layout map, as illustrated in Figure 5.14, and estimates the distance of each flow path, the required walking time, and the yearly frequency of such paths. From this information, he calculates the number of miles annually covered by employees moving among the various workstations, as well as estimated annual walking times. He concludes that employees are walking approximately 380 miles per year at an annual time of some 550 hours!

As shown in Figure 5.14, what appears to be a very neat, precise, and orderly work layout is actually very inefficient. The present layout configuration continuously interrupts work flow by forcing employees to constantly carry work from one machine to another. In addition, by having all machines facing in the same direction, employees must walk around machines in rather circuitous and inefficient routes.

Further, the highest frequency flow paths require employees to walk the farthest distances. For example, work stations #1 and #6 are the farthest apart. Yet this flow path occurs 45 percent of the time. Although times associated with any individual transportation step are rather minor, cumulative times quickly add up because of the extremely high frequencies associated with the process. In fact, the consultant estimates that about 20 percent of the time is spent in the non-value-adding activity of carrying work from one machine to another or retrieving needed supplies from distant storage cabinets.

The location and organization of the supply cabinets also cause numerous interruptions in work flow. Supplies, although neatly arranged, are not grouped according to frequency of use. Through additional observation, the consultant is able to group supplies into two major categories: those required on a daily basis and those needed only on a weekly basis. Currently, each supply cabinet contains a mixture of supplies used both daily and weekly. This intermixing requires employees to look through all of the cabinets in order to retrieve needed supplies.

To reduce cycle times and improve continuous work flow, the consultant suggests rearranging the work stations in a cellular fashion (Figure 5.15). The new design proposes placing work station #1 directly across from and facing work station #6, since this represents the highest frequency flow path (45 percent of the time). He would then place work station #4 directly next to work station #6. This represents the second highest frequency flow path (30 percent of the time). Seventy-five percent of the work could now be done within one confined area, eliminating the need to constantly walk back and forth among the three most frequently used machines. He also proposes arranging the other machines to mimic the two remaining flow paths. For example, he would place work station #5 directly across from work station #3 and work station #2 next to work station #1.

In addition, the consultant suggests reorganizing and rearranging storage cabinets based on frequency of use. Two cabinets containing supplies only used on a daily basis would be placed in the immediate

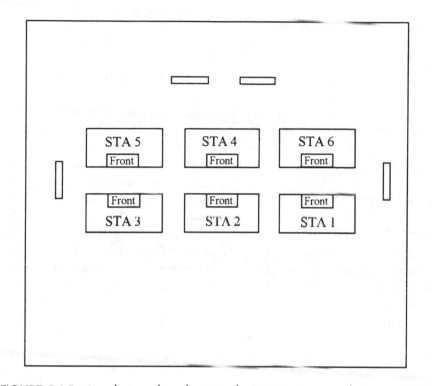

FIGURE 5.15. A redesigned work station layout. Compare with Figure 5.13.

work area. One supply cabinet would support work stations #1, 4, and 6. The second cabinet would support work stations #2, 3, and 5. Supplies needed on a weekly basis would be placed behind the cellular layout. The new process layout is expected to decrease required transportation (walking) distances from 380 miles to 80 miles per year and time spent moving among the machines and supply cabinets will be reduced from 550 hours (almost 69 days) to 85 hours (some 10.5 days) annually. Both sets of numbers represent an approximate reduction of well over 80 percent. Delay times associated with searching through multiple cabinets to retrieve needed supplies will also be significantly reduced. Total expected annual time savings is estimated to be some 700 hours per year.

The consultant presents his observations and suggestions to the businessman interested in purchasing the printing company. He suggests that, with very little effort and almost no cost, at least a 15 to

20 percent increase in productivity could be obtained per shift. This productivity improvement would be accomplished by decreasing the amount of time it takes to process a customer's order. Reducing cycle time would be accomplished by improving continuous work flow via improved process layout.

Furthermore, the number of employees required to operate the machines could be reduced because the machines would be more easily accessible. One person, for example, could easily attend the three machines that account for 75 percent of the work, which are presently being attended by two employees. If excess employees could be placed on an additional second shift, store hours could be significantly extended at very little additional cost. For example, the store could remain open from 7:00 am to 11:00 pm, as opposed to its current 9:00 am to 5:00 pm hours of operation. This in turn would significantly increase profitability as current and estimated work load would easily support the proposed extended work hours.

The businessman is very pleased with the consultant's recommendations. He's also a little embarrassed that he missed seeing any of these potential areas for improvement himself. Quite frankly, he thought it was a very efficient and well laid out operation. What he failed to realize, however, was that the numerous little inefficiencies and interruptions in work flow can quickly add up to major inefficiencies. This observation is especially true in very high-frequency work environments like the printing business.

Convinced that significant increases in profitability can be achieved, the businessman rates the company in the high/high sector of his decision table. He decides to proceed with the purchase of the company. One year later, he's very glad that he did. All of the suggested improvements made by the consultant were immediately implemented following the closing of the sale with almost no additional costs. Productivity, along with profitability, substantially increased. And best of all, business continues to grow. In fact, the businessman is now considering opening up two additional stores in surrounding areas.

SUMMARY

A key objective in any cycle time reduction initiative is to create continuous process flow. In continuous flow, products, materials, information, goods, people, and just about everything else move continuously, stopping only when value is directly being added. In continuous flow, all process steps become interdependent elements of a larger, single process, seamlessly connected. As such, it does little good to improve only a portion of a process. Instead, all parts must be improved and integrated into a continuously flowing whole.

To achieve the ideal of continuous work flow and associated theoretical cycle times, all unnecessary delays and other non-value-adding steps must be identified and completely eliminated. All required resources also must be immediately available and accessible at the right time and place. In many instances, technology can be a powerful ally in improving continuous process flow.

Achieving continuous flow is commonly impeded by the presence of a few significant delays that represent major process chokepoints. Often, only a few such delays can account for a disproportionate amount of total process cycle time. Identifying and either eliminating or significantly minimizing these major chokepoints is critical then to improving overall process flow. Sometimes such chokepoints are caused by work volumes exceeding the capacity limitations of available human and machine resources. At other times, periodic work surges may temporarily strain existing resource capacities, thereby interrupting process flow. Work leveling can sometimes help moderate such volume surges. Finally, the physical layout of a work process can cause numerous interruptions and delays in a process. By better aligning work layout to mimic process flow and high-frequency flow paths, significant reductions in cycle times can be achieved.

6 CROSS-FUNCTIONAL — WORK TEAMS

An important element in any cycle time reduction initiative is the ability to effectively coordinate work activities and the humans associated with those activities. In many instances, process delays are caused by our inability to successfully coordinate work activities at company division or departmental levels. As will be discussed, there are a multitude of reasons for these limitations. Many, however, center around the very nature of human cooperation itself. Indeed, in too many companies, interdivisional and interdepartmental cooperation falls along a continuum bordering somewhere between resigned tolerance and open hostility!

In some instances, the prudent use of cross-functional work teams can reduce the need for such close cooperation. A cross-functional work team describes a small group of individuals representing diverse disciplines and departments, who are focused solely on completing a specific work activity or group of related work activities in the most efficient and effective manner possible.

One major manufacturer of power tools, appliances, and home security products has speeded up its new product development process by organizing into cross-functional teams composed of design engineers, production managers, and marketers. The teams work on an entire family of new products from their inception. The team focuses on identifying ways to standardize components among several new products to make them easier and less costly to assemble. Such improvements have reportedly[1] cut the cost and time of new product development in half.

To better understand the potential role of cross-functional work teams in reducing cycle time, it is first important to understand the sometimes conflicting relationship between processes and organization structures.

ORGANIZATIONS AND PROCESSES

Organizations typically configure themselves around functions and related disciplines. For example, an organization involved in the manufacturing of a particular group of products may have an engineering division, a manufacturing division, a marketing division, a sales division, a shipping division, and so on. Within each division are grouped related disciplines. For instance, the engineering division represents a grouping of engineering-related disciplines. To differentiate itself further, the engineering division may subdivide itself into more narrowly defined disciplines such as an electrical engineering department staffed with electrical engineers, a mechanical engineering department staffed with mechanical engineers, and an industrial engineering department staffed with industrial engineers. In each department, personnel are engaged in some type of specific, discipline-related work.

On the basis of such functional and discipline-related categories, organizations structure themselves around functions typically represented by company divisions. In turn, divisions are configured around departmental disciplines. Subgroups within a department are configured around still narrower defined discipline specialties. This commonly used division-department-section hierarchy is graphically depicted in Figure 6.1.

As a consequence of this organizational approach, we end up with companies being comprised of numerous groups that represent various disciplines, subdisciplines, and even sub-subdisciplines. The various groups typically reside in individual and isolated division locations or "silos." This typical silo approach to organizational design is

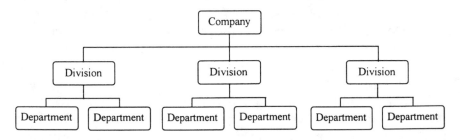

FIGURE 6.1. A typical company organizational chart.

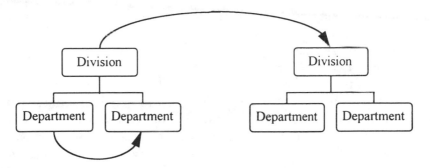

FIGURE 6.2. Work is normally handed off from department to department, and division to division.

illustrated in Figure 6.2. Under such organizational configurations, work is done within specific, discipline-related groups. When the work is completed in one group, it is often handed off to another group within an individual silo or even to another silo for further processing. In this way, work is accomplished.

In other instances, isolated groups may work on a particular activity in parallel. Each group's independent outputs are then blended together to form some final, integrated output. Sometimes this blending effort is successful, sometimes it isn't. In either case, it is almost always accompanied by numerous inefficiencies. Also, such narrowly restricted and isolated views of work can often cause subsequent problems.

For example, engineering may design a product with little or no input from those charged with manufacturing or distributing the product. As a result, unnecessary constraints are built into manufacturing and distribution right from the beginning that will adversely affect cycle time further along in the process stream. Such downstream difficulties can be illustrated by the following scenario.

The engineering division of a large company designed a new product. Components for the new product are produced and then assembled by manufacturing. During the initial product design phase, individual groups within engineering were tasked with designing the individual components. These independent designs were then integrated into a final product design. During the course of the design effort, each group unknowingly selected a different sized bolt and accompanying washer and nut for attaching its specific component during the final assembly phase.

As a result of such individual selections, those actually doing the final assembly now have to constantly retrieve different sized bolts, nuts, and washers, as well as different sized tools. These repeated retrieval steps in turn increase assembly cycle time. In addition, separate inventories have to be ordered and maintained for each sized bolt, nut, and washer. Interestingly, there was no specific reason for why a more standardized bolt could not have been used for the final assembly of all of the components. However, poor communication within engineering, and the complete lack of communication between engineering and manufacturing, caused no one to consider such an insignificant detail. This oversight in engineering unnecessarily cost manufacturing increased assembly cycle times.

Besides divisions and departments, companies also have associated processes. Normally a company has a unique set of processes that capture all of their associated work activities. However, the configuration of these processes usually bears little resemblance to the configuration of the company's organizational structure. That is, a company's organizational chart bears little resemblance to its process chart, and that's why problems occur, especially problems related to cycle time.

Processes almost always cut across vertically aligned and isolated divisions and departments. This horizontal cross-cutting relationship is illustrated in Figure 6.3, which depicts three processes cutting across the boundaries of four separate division silos. As a result of such cross-cutting relationships, discontinuities form between a company's organizational structure and its process structure.

A common outcome of this structural disequilibrium is that process-related delays develop at divisional and departmental boundaries. As a result, process flow is interrupted and cycle time is increased. Process boundaries that ideally should be seamlessly connected become instead, jagged, poorly fitting junctures. This fragmented process condition is depicted graphically in Figure 6.4. Although work may flow fairly efficiently within each process "chunk" illustrated in Figure 6.4, overall process flow is greatly impeded.

It is perhaps noteworthy to observe that in most organizations no one is tasked with managing an entire process—no one actually owns a process. No one has the responsibility and authority for assur-

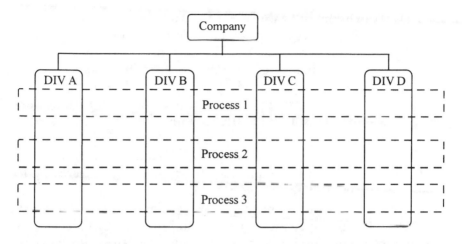

FIGURE 6.3. Processes normally cut across divisional boundaries.

ing that overall process flow is maintained and that the individual parts function in an integrated, efficient whole. Instead, everyone owns and manages a piece of the process, as depicted by an individual process chunk in Figure 6.4. Consequently, organizational-related delays are an almost inevitable byproduct of large, companywide processes.

Disruptions and resultant delays at organizational boundaries can occur for a number of reasons. Sometimes it's caused by differing work priorities, when work is placed on hold within a division or department for other, more pressing priorities. As a result, work flow is interrupted and delays ensue. Sometimes, poor communication results in not contacting the right people or not providing the right information at the right time—things just fall through the cracks.

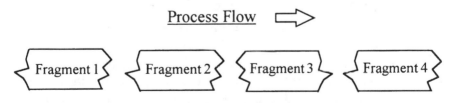

FIGURE 6.4. A fragmented and poorly connected flow process. As a result, overall flow is interrupted at individual boundaries.

Delays can also result from an overt or unconscious unwillingness to cooperate. Such unwilling cooperation can be caused by a number of things, including company politics, interdivisional rivalries, personal agendas, or management infighting. In some instances, competitive rivalries among divisions are set up purposely to supposedly spur performance. Although such incentives may improve performance within divisions, it does little to improve performance for the company as a whole.

At still other times, delays result from bureaucratic inefficiencies. Things simply go into a bureaucratic "black hole" and never seem to come out again. Whatever the reason, the outcome is often the same—slow and costly company processes. This outcome can result despite the fact that individual divisions and departments are actually working in an efficient and cost-effective manner. Although the individual parts of the process may be performing well, they still are not connected into an efficient, integrated whole. This results in overall process flow being continuously interrupted.

Unfortunately, there are no magical cures for the realities of organizational structures and processes. Every organizational configuration has both its strengths and weaknesses. The creation and selective use of cross-functional work teams can prove highly effective, however, especially if a major goal is to eliminate delays associated with disjointed cross-functional boundaries.

CROSS-FUNCTIONAL WORK TEAMS

The general manager at a large plant complex became increasingly irritated with his management staff for their inability to meet scheduled commitments. It seemed that everything was taking too long. This inefficiency resulted in a continuous stream of overdue commitments coming across his desk. Finally and in frustration, the general manager held an all-management meeting in which he spent considerable time berating his managers for their inabilities to meet scheduled commitments. He told the assembled group that he held each of them personally responsible for the company's poor and slow performance and demanded immediate improvement. If they couldn't learn to work faster, threatened the general manager, perhaps they could learn to work elsewhere!

During the hour-long berating, the angry general manager asked some rather insightful questions. Why is it, he asked, that whenever he puts together a special project team whose membership is drawn from diverse divisions and departments, things get done in a hurry? Why can't ordinary division and department managers make the same kinds of things happen as quickly? Why does it seem to always take a special team or task force?

It's suggested that if this particular manager would have reflected upon his posed questions, he may have discovered some interesting insights. He may have discovered why cross-functional teams frequently work when functional departments and divisions don't. He may have even discovered that a great deal of a cross-functional team's success may not necessarily be tied solely to the use of teams, as is so often thought. Rather, success may actually be associated more with organizing people around a specific work activity itself and focusing them on completing that activity.

As noted previously, a process is often comprised of a series of interrelated work activities. Activities, in turn, are comprised of a series of process steps. Successfully accomplishing a work activity or group of activities often requires multiple personnel from multiple divisions and departments. These required human resources further represent multiple disciplines. A traditional, functionally-structured organization basically dictates that work be passed back and forth among various groups. This constant handoff is illustrated graphically in Figure 6.5. Unfortunately, at each required handoff, there is a possibility that a resultant delay will occur.

This situation is somewhat analogous to the running of a relay race at a track meet in which the successful and speedy handoff of the baton from one team member to another is as critical to winning the race as is running as fast as possible. A slow handoff can cost precious seconds that may ultimately determine the difference between winning and losing. The speed at which an organization passes work back and forth among multiple groups is also greatly dependent upon the efficiency of the handoff. Just like the track example, slow handoffs lengthen cycle time.

If we focus on the work itself and not the functional grouping of disciplines required to do the work, we find something quite different. By focusing on work first, the nature of the work activity often dictates required personnel resources. It also can help us understand

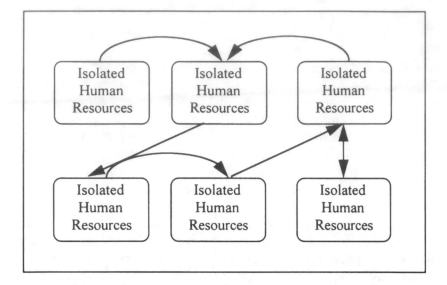

FIGURE 6.5. Work is frequently passed back and forth among individuals or groups of individuals in a very complex manner. Frequently delays occur at handoff points, resulting in an interrupted process flow.

the best way to configure those human resources. If we subdivide a large process into various work activity levels, a type of organizational chart not unlike a traditional organizational chart, appears as illustrated in Figure 6.6. However, this type of organizational chart, is associated with completing specific work activities. It is not associated with trying to define artificial boundaries among various disciplines.

Returning to the irate general manager discussed earlier, the reason why his company experienced such great success with special project teams was because the teams' focus was on completing a well-defined work activity within a set time frame. The work itself dictated who should be assigned to the team. With all required personnel represented on the team, the need for interdepartmental handoffs simply disappeared.

Also, there was a unified team focus dictated by the activity itself. No longer were personnel there to perform only a specific discipline. Rather, they were there to focus their unique talents on completing a specific work activity as quickly as possible. Although this distinction

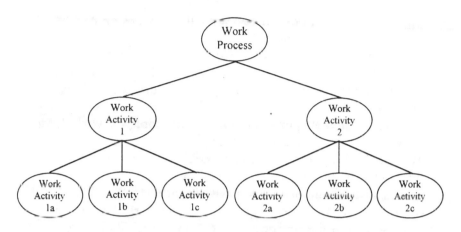

FIGURE 6.6. An "organizational" chart associated with work itself.

may seem rather trivial, it's not. It possibly may be a critical insight to more efficiently organizing people and work.

It is suggested that, all too frequently, we seem to forget the real purpose of our jobs, and that is to focus our energies on accomplishing a specific work activity in the most efficient and effective manner possible. By intelligently using multidisciplined, cross-functional work teams supplied with all needed resources to complete a specific work activity, that focus stands a better chance of being understood. However, this observation does not mean to imply that teams are the answer to everything. Just like technology, work teams are basically neutral. It's how we use them that counts. Simply putting together a team will not in itself guarantee reduced cycle times anymore than merely using a new piece of technology. Only the prudent use of work teams can positively affect work flow.

When used wisely, cross-functional work teams have much to offer an organization as a means of increasing process speed. This is especially true of cross-functional teams whose membership is drawn from diverse divisions and departments on an as-needed basis, and whose sole focus is directed towards completing a specific work activity in a cooperative and efficient manner.

However, the successful application of cross-functional work teams may not depend solely on a company's ability to create an effective team environment. It may also be dependent on its ability to successfully define and design work itself. This design capability includes correctly identifying all associated work activities and all required resources, as well as coordinating those activities and resources in an effective and efficient manner. Indeed, our ability to successfully design work and creatively configure required resources to accomplish that work may well determine our success in obtaining needed economies of speed. The important topic of work design is covered in much greater detail in Chapter 7.

If companies can define specific work activities complete with associated performance parameters, they can wisely use cross-functional work teams to accomplish those activities quickly. This observation, however, is based on the assumption that managers will actually relinquish personnel in their respective groups to participate in such team settings. In many instances, work teams are more fictional than real. Team members really still haven't left the confines of their individual division silos. In some instances, this can be attributed to unparticipative or unwilling managers who believe that personal turf and fiefdom building is more important than company success.

In other instances, employees themselves are unwilling to participate on cross-functional work teams. This is particularly interesting and offers some real challenges to the design of work in the coming years. In many cases, the use of cross-functional teams is simply not acceptable to many individuals. We've created such a climate of discipline-related allegiances that individuals identify with a specific discipline or discipline-related work group more strongly than they do with the company they're working for. Accepting this reality, we must rethink the whole issue of organization and job design if we are to generate a more cooperative, multidisciplined, and faster approach to accomplishing work. For some thoughtful insights into the many issues involved in organizational and job design, the reader is referred to the work of William Bridges. Indeed, the whole concept of jobs as we know them today is seriously challenged by Bridges in his book, *JobShift*.[2]

It is suggested then that the judicious use of cross-functional work teams that contain all needed personnel resources and are focused on completing a specific work activity or group of related activities can greatly accelerate cycle times. The whole topic of using cross-functional work teams has received wide coverage over the past few years under numerous names, including concurrent and simultaneous engineering. Regardless of the descriptive name used, however, the goal is the same; to use a cooperative, multidisciplined, team environment to complete a specific project or work activity in the most efficient and effective manner possible.

The following generic case study illustrates the potential application of cross-functional work teams in accelerating the speed of work. As described in the case study, the logical use of such teams and the acceptance by involved individuals, however, are two very different things.

CASE STUDY #5

An environmental company was awarded a government contract to characterize and remedy a hazardous waste site. A recent government audit of the firm's performance, however, produced a scathing report. The report concluded that ". . . little if any substantial progress has been made during the initial two-year effort." Stung by the report's criticism and concerned that the company's lucrative contract may be prematurely terminated, a corporate management team was assembled and dispatched to the site. The team consisted of five senior managers and one outside consultant.

An initial meeting with government oversight personnel was held. The oversight personnel indicated that although the quality of the work being performed by the company is satisfactory, the pace of the work is dismal. One government official noted that, ". . . even a snail's pace would be a big improvement." In short, it seemed that it simply took too long for the company to do anything. The corporate management team realized that it must do something quickly if it was to improve the company's performance record and reputation.

To better utilize team expertise and time, different assignments were given to each team member. The outside consultant on the team was tasked with reviewing the company's organizational structure at the site. She was to determine if the organizational configuration was impeding work efficiency. The consultant is a well recognized expert in this area. Her philosophy is that although there is never a perfect organizational structure, there is commonly an optimal structure for a given organizational goal.

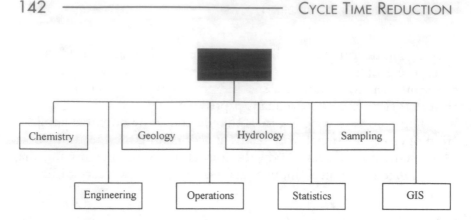

FIGURE 6.7. The original organizational chart for the environmental company. Examining the chart, can you tell specifically what the company does?

The consultant asked for a current organization chart. A long time ago, she learned a useful and very insightful trick. Upon receiving the chart, she took a black marking pen and blackened out the top box. This altered organizational chart is graphically depicted in Figure 6.7. She then asked herself, "What is the specific purpose of this organization?" Looking at the chart, she saw a number of departmental disciplines. These included Geology, Hydrology, Statistics, Chemistry, and Engineering. If one didn't know any better, the consultant concluded, the chart almost resembled a college curriculum for a technical degree program. Interestingly, the general manager at the site is a former college professor.

Armed with this initial observation, the consultant began examining the various departments. She first received an overview of each department from the respective department manager. Then she randomly interviewed company personnel working in each department. All of the interviews included a similar set of questions. What is your job? What is the purpose of your job? What major process are you a part of? How do you interact and coordinate your activities with other departments? What is the purpose of the company being here? What is the company's immediate goal?

Responses to the questions were surprisingly similar. Everyone seemed to view their job from the specific discipline they represent. That is, "I'm a hydrologist" or "I'm an engineer" or "I'm a statistician." In turn, they answer the "what-is-the-purpose-of-your-job" question with "to do hydrology" or "to do engineering" or "to do statistics." No one seemed to know anything about processes or the company's purpose or goal.

As far as interacting with other departments, the response was fairly uniform with a "we really don't" reply. One person in the sampling department told her that he often takes the same samples for different departments. "Don't these people ever talk to each other or coordinate their efforts?", he asked her.

The consultant next examined the cleanup task the company is charged with. It seemed the hazardous waste site was dotted with a series of toxic "hot spots." The toxic hot spots were spread over thousands of acres and grouped into well defined geographical areas. Each defined area is called an Operational Unit or "OU" for short. There were seven defined OUs at the site, identified as OU1, OU2, OU3, etc.

The company was hired to characterize and remedy these seven OUs. With final remediation comes OU closure which is the purpose of the company being there. The goal of the company was to close the OUs as cost effectively and quickly as possible. Unfortunately, management never shared this information with anyone. The consultant wasn't even sure whether management had shared this with management! So instead of working on OU closure, departments simply worked on geology, hydrology, chemistry, etc. Employees had no defined focus or overall goal to work toward.

Further study indicated that there were similarities and differences among the seven OUs. However, the OUs could be conveniently clustered into four distinct groups. These include OUs 1 and 4, OUs 2 and 6, OUs 3 and 5, and OU7.

The consultant later met with other members of the management team. One team member concluded that there were no well-defined processes in place. "Everyone just kind of does his or her own thing," he remarked. There also was no commonly shared information base. People seemed to hoard information within each department, not wanting to share it with anyone. Also, every department seemed to have its own unique and totally different information gathering, storage, and distribution system.

The consultant was then asked for her input. She concluded that interdepartmental cooperation and coordination were almost nonexistent and it seemed as if no one realized the real purpose and goal of the company. That purpose and goal, she reminded everyone on the management team, was to close out the seven OUs as quickly and cost effectively as possible. One senior manager sarcastically remarked, "Isn't that obvious to everyone?" "No it's not," replied the consultant, "and that's a big part of your problem here. No one knows what this project is all about."

The consultant suggested a major reorganization followed by a redesign of all core work processes. Some on the management team questioned why every company problem must always be resolved by yet another reorganization. Why not just fix the broken processes? The consultant agreed that reorganizing isn't always the right answer. It can sometimes even make things worse. In this case, however, she thought reorganizing would result in an immediate improvement. It would focus people on the real job, which is OU closure.

She suggested developing four cross-functional or multidiscipline work teams dedicated to completing a specific work activity and would parallel the four OU groupings. The teams would be called OU 1 & 4 Closure Team, OU2 & 6 Closure Team, OU 3 & 5 Closure Team, and OU 7 Closure Team. Each team's sole responsibility and focus would be to close their respective OUs as quickly and cost effectively as possible. One other team would be called the OU Closure Support Team. This team would house some of the site's shared capabilities, such as the GIS database. The new suggested organizational structure is depicted graphically in Figure 6.8. As illustrated, it is built around five cross-functional work teams.

There was still a great deal of skepticism among the other team members. To reinforce her suggestions, the consultant had each team member compare the before and after organizational charts, as illustrated in Figures 6.7 and 6.8 respectively. Just on the basis of the charts, she asked the team members to describe the specific purpose of the organization. The answer was perfectly clear for the new chart: OU closure. However, no one could discern the specific purpose from the old chart. Almost immediately, the other team members understood the consultant's point of view.

The team spent considerable time thoughtfully discussing the pros and cons of the new organizational structure. They further discussed in a general fashion who and what should go where. One concern voiced was that the four different OU closure teams might go in four completely different directions. The team concluded that with standard work processes in place, much of this individualism could be

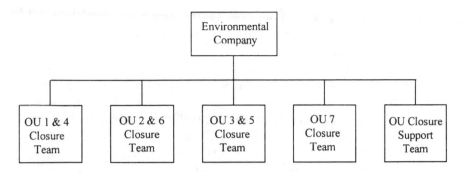

FIGURE 6.8. The reconfigured organization focusing on OU closure.

avoided. Other issues also surfaced, but, one by one each was re-solved satisfactorily. Finally, everyone agreed that a major reorganiza-tion around cross-functional work teams was an important first step in the right direction. Each newly formed work team would focus solely on completing OU closures as quickly and cost effectively as possible.

The outside management team held a meeting with all of the on-site managers. Although the team tried to work with local manage-ment in as cordial manner as possible, there was still a great deal of suspicion and uneasiness. There also was a pervasive feeling among the onsite managers that everything really was okay, that they really weren't in any jeopardy of losing their contract.

The team presented all of its findings in a very systematic, fact-based manner. The outside consultant was then asked to present her findings and suggestions. After reviewing all of her collected informa-tion with the onsite managers, she passed out a draft organizational chart. She reviewed the proposed reorganization and asked for the managers' initial thoughts and comments. Surprisingly, there was lit-tle disagreement with the overall logic behind the restructuring ratio-nale. One manager noted, "I really don't like it but I have to admit, it actually does make good sense." With the local managers' help and input, additional changes were made.

The next day, the general manager held a companywide meeting with all onsite employees to discuss the team's findings and talk about the proposed reorganization. Many people in the audience were adamantly opposed to the idea. They felt their allegiances were to their at-present group. They were also concerned that they would become isolated from their colleagues and academic disciplines. Another general complaint was, "What will I put on my resumé? That I was an OU Closure Team member!"

The general manager was somewhat surprised at how personally many employees were taking the suggested reorganization. For the first time he saw that no one at the site really was thinking about the company's primary mission; to close OUs as quickly and cost effectively as possible. It was evident to him that he had failed to communicate this mission to anyone. In the past, he simply took for granted that everyone knew the company's purpose for being there. He realized, however, that he was mistaken in making this assumption.

Realizing that he must start somewhere, he reiterated to the employees that each of their individual needs were very important. So was the reason for why the company was awarded the contract in the first place. As such, he thought reorganizing around OU-related cross-functional work teams was a good idea. He asked for their help, input, and continued support.

The teams were formed over the next few weeks. The title of "project" something was given to all team members, for example, project chemist, project geologist, project engineer. This seemed to soothe the "resumé" concerns. Although things didn't instantly start getting better, everyone soon realized that the reorganization was actually a pretty good idea. For the first time, team members were focusing their combined disciplinary talents and efforts on OU closure.

Six months later, the results were encouraging. There weren't any overnight miracles or instant success stories, but day by day, things began to improve. Actual work started getting done at a much faster pace. Oversight personnel, representing the immediate customer, were extremely pleased with the new progress. As one government official was quoted as saying, "It's amazing what can be done when we focus the right group of people on accomplishing a specific work activity."

SUMMARY

The realities of horizontally oriented processes and vertically oriented and isolated company divisions and departments frequently result in ensuing process-related delays at organizational boundaries. In some instances, the use of cross-functional work teams can eliminate such organizationally induced delays.

A cross-functional work team can be described as the following:

- a small group of individuals,

- representing diverse disciplines and departments, who are

- focused solely on completing a specific work activity or group of related work activities,

- in the most efficient and effective manner possible.

The success experienced using cross-functional teams, however, may not only be related to using a team-based approach per se. Rather, the real key may be in attempting to configure and focus human effort around a specific work activity itself.

7 ──── ACTIVITY-BASED ──── WORK DESIGN

The previous five chapters have focused on reducing the cycle time of existing processes and work activities. A key concept in such endeavors is the identification and subsequent elimination, or at least minimization, of all non-value-adding process steps that add only delay and additional cost. Eliminating or minimizing process waste can be accomplished through a variety of means, from ensuring immediate resource availability and accessibility, to better utilizing technology and cross-functional work teams.

In this chapter, we'll turn our attention from reducing the cycle time of an existing process and begin focusing on the initial design of a new process or work activity. The emphasis will be on preventing non-value-adding process steps from being built into a process or work activity in the first place. That is, the emphasis will be on designing lean, simple processes devoid of unnecessary and time-consuming delays.

A recent and valid criticism of the process reengineering movement is that it makes a false assumption. By using the term reengineering, we imply that a process was initially engineered to begin with and that process redesign logically follows process design. In most instances, little process engineering or design actually takes place. Instead, processes seem to evolve haphazardly with little forethought or control. They also seem to grow, get bigger, and become more complex through time. As a result of this almost continuous exponential growth rate, value-adding process steps quickly become lost in a sea of non-value-adding steps and activities.

Many current processes also evolved prior to the pervasive use of computer-based technologies. Little has been done to fundamentally rethink process design, and the whole concept of work itself for that matter, in the information age.

What's the reason for this pervasive absence of initial process design? It's suggested that it's because we seem to focus our efforts on designing operations, not processes. Most flow charts and accompanying procedures depict an operational design, not a process design, and unfortunately, the design of an operation does not equate with the design of a process.

It is further suggested that this lack of initial process design is a result of how we view work itself. When viewing work, we almost always tend to focus our attention on what people or machines are doing to something. That is, only operation steps are observed and considered. When we design work, we do exactly the same thing. We only design operation steps. Little attention is given to the design of the overall process, or what actually happens in between all of the operation steps. For example, we never consider all of the transportation, delay, inspection, storage, and rework steps that accompany most operation steps. As a result of this common oversight, we usually end up doing a good job of designing operations, but a poor job of designing processes. Unfortunately, such poor process designs result in some very undesirable and often predictable consequences.

One commonly encountered problem associated with inadequate process design is our inability to properly schedule work. Despite the use of sophisticated scheduling software programs, many companies still experience numerous problems in successfully scheduling work activities. One reason for this recurring problem is simply the dynamic and constantly changing environment that most of us work in today. Another suggested reason is that companies fail to adequately design and schedule at the process level.

An operation step may take only 60 minutes to complete, yet the delay and transportation steps associated with this single operation step may actually take two to three days. Although we properly identify the required operation step and correctly schedule the 60 minutes, we often fail to consider and include the accompanying two to three days of delay and transportation steps. As a result of such process oversights, carefully planned operations-based work schedules quickly fall behind. The real problem in such instances may not be in our inability to schedule work, but in our inability to design work in the first place. The real problem also may not be in our inability to design an operation, but in our inability to design a process.

In the following sections we'll explore process design as opposed to operations design. Specifically, we'll concentrate our efforts on preventing process delays from initially occurring. Much of our design efforts will focus on the work activity level. Before proceeding, however, it's important to recognize that the same basic principles discussed in reducing the cycle time of an existing process are still applicable to the design of a new process or work activity. Remember, these basic principles are:

- Eliminate process waste.

- Provide the right resources at the right place and time.

- Use technology to improve process flow.

- Create continuous work flow.

- Use cross-functional teams focused on completing a specific work activity.

WORK ACTIVITIES

As noted in Chapter 2, a process represents the blending and transformation of a set of inputs into a more valuable set of outputs. Outputs, which go to either internal or external customers, represent products and services. Processes, especially large processes, can frequently be divided conveniently into a series of interrelated work activities. A work activity, just like a process, has a clearly defined beginning and end, as well as a specific output. This decomposition of a process into various associated work activities is graphically illustrated in Figure 7.1.

When designing a large process, it is often much easier to work at the activity level than it is at the process level. This approach, however, does not mean that work activities are designed in isolation from each other. Instead, they must be designed as interrelated and integrated supporting modules of the larger overall process. Adopting such an integrated, modular approach assures that activities are designed to support overall process flow, as well as to optimize work activity connectiveness.

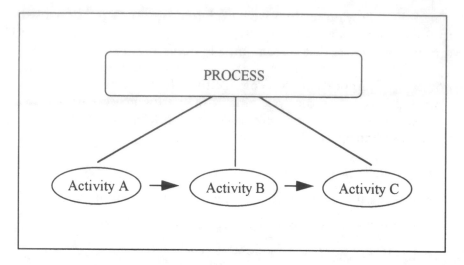

FIGURE 7.1. A large process can frequently be divided into a series of interrelated work activities.

An activity then can be viewed as representing a major segment of work directed towards achieving a specific output. A work activity in turn supports the overall goal, purpose, and output of a larger process. Activities, therefore, should always directly add value to any process. Work activities must always be performed to accomplish a specific process supporting goal. They must also be conducted within a specified set of performance parameters (e.g., cost, quality, time, productivity, safety). Finally, work activities must be performed to satisfy an internal or external customer, just like the larger process in which they are part of.

Typically, a work activity is accomplished by a group of people. Although the size of the group can vary, group size is usually somewhere between two to 15 individuals. The degree of required interaction and coordination among these individuals, however, can vary greatly. In some instances, a highly coordinated and choreographed cross-functional work team is required. In other situations, a much lesser degree of coordination is needed and people can work more or less independently of each other. In such instances, they really aren't a team, but instead a group of independently working individuals.

Work activities consume or use resources other than just people. Many work activities consume materials, supplies, equipment, external services, and information. Information can flow directly into a work activity from an outside source. It can also be generated within an activity and flow outward to other associated activities. Work activities also frequently require some type of physical space and/or facility. Some of the various characteristics of a work activity are depicted graphically in Figure 7.2.

Products and services, which represent final process outputs, can be thought of as consuming work activities. In turn, work activities consume resources. Because activities consume precious and increasingly scarce working capital, eliminating non-value-adding work activities and non-value-adding process steps within an activity is extremely important if we are to better leverage company funds.

Work activities can normally be categorized under three general headings: continuous, intermittent, and virtual. Continuous work activities are performed on an ongoing basis while intermittent activities are performed only on a periodic basis. Periodicity may occur on a set or random schedule. Finally, virtual activities are usually unique,

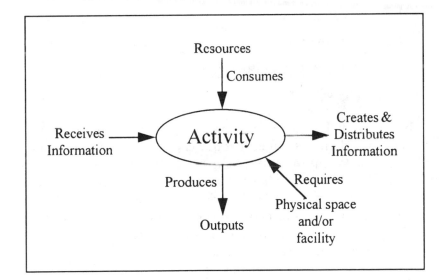

FIGURE 7.2. Some basic characteristics of a work activity.

one-time-only activities. A large work process, depending on its complexity and branching pathways, may include one, two, or even all three types of work activities.

Work activities are also related to each other in various ways. Some work activities are directly related, with one activity triggering one or more other subsequent work activities. That is, there is a dependent and precursor relationship among the activities. In other instances, activities can be largely independent of each other, occurring in parallel. Although they may be supporting the same process, there is little if any direct interaction.

To illustrate these various interactions, the turnaround process of a commercial jet at a major airport can be viewed as consisting of a series of interrelated work activities. Some of these major activities include:

- Parking aircraft.

- Unloading passengers.

- Unloading baggage.

- Servicing aircraft.

- Loading passengers.

- Loading baggage.

- Conducting preflight inspection.

- Launching aircraft.

In our example, loading passengers cannot begin until passengers are first unloaded. Passenger loading is dependent upon passenger unloading occurring first. In this instance, unloading passengers is the precursor to loading passengers. Furthermore, passenger loading is an independent and parallel activity of servicing aircraft. Both activities are related to and directly support the jet turnaround process. Finally, all activities must precede launching aircraft. Launching aircraft represents a successor activity to all other activities.

Based on this initial understanding of a work activity, we can begin the initial design of a work process. Our design effort will be divided into three major segments. Although presented in a linear fashion, the segments are normally conducted in an iterative, "circular" fashion. The three major design segments are the following:

- Initial process characterization, which focuses on gathering basic information at the process level.

- Activity-based work design, which focuses on designing individual work activities and all associated process steps, as well as identifying all required resources.

- Activity integration, which focuses on assuring the optimal integration of all individual work activities so that a cohesive and well-coordinated process whole forms.

Each of these major design segments will be described in greater detail in the following three sections.

INITIAL PROCESS CHARACTERIZATION

The purpose of this first design phase is to develop basic information and design criteria, as well as determine various performance parameters at the process level. To begin our initial design effort at the process level, we must first define the following:

- The purpose and goal of the proposed process.

- Its specific outputs and receiving customers, whether internal or external.

- The perceived value of the process and outputs to the receiving customer. We must determine whether perceived customer value is low, moderate, or high. If perceived value is determined to be low, we must seriously question why we need the process in the first place.

- The performance parameters within which the process must be conducted (e.g., time, cost, productivity, quality, throughput levels, customer expectations).

- Any regulatory or legal constraints that may affect the design of the process.

- Any technological considerations that may constrain or enhance process design.

After completing this initial process characterization, we can then divide a proposed process into a series of interrelated work activities. In some instances, people may experience problems initially identifying specific process-related work activities. A good technique to use in such situations is to first develop an activity cluster diagram. To construct an activity cluster diagram, which is sometimes referred to as an affinity diagram, complete the following steps.

1. Brainstorm all of the things one has to do to successfully complete a process. Record each idea on individual note cards. The level of detail is not important at this point, nor is any logical order required. Just record anything that pops into people's minds. Usually, a small group of four to five people work best for developing an activity cluster diagram.

2. Place all of the completed note cards on a large, flat surface. Then cluster them into related groups. That is, simply have people place the cards into like or related groupings.

3. Identify each group with a header card. A header card includes a title that best captures the central idea that ties all of the other note cards in the group together.

4. Examine the header cards and see if anything has been left out. If so, add as needed.

5. Record all of the header cards. The header cards represent an initial identification of individual work activities.

As the process design progresses, some of the identified work activities may be changed or eliminated. Others may also be added.

In some instances, a process is small enough that additional decomposition into work activities is unnecessary. The process can basically be treated as a single work activity. If this is the case, proceed directly to the second design segment—activity-based work design.

Once activities have been identified, we can list them in a table. We also should classify their precursor and temporal interrelationships, as well as activity type (continuous, intermittent, and virtual). Also,

TABLE 7.1. ACTIVITY CATEGORIZATION MATRIX

#	Activity	Precursor Relationship	Continuous	Intermittent	Virtual
1	Parking aircraft	Must precede all other activities (#2 through #8)	X		
2	Unload passengers	Preceded by Activity #1	X		
3	Unload baggage	Preceded by Activity #1	X		
4	Load passengers	Preceded by Activity #1, then Activity #2	X		
5	Load baggage	Preceded by Activity #1, then Activity #3	X		
6	Service aircraft	Preceded by Activity #1	X		
7	Conduct preflight	Preceded by Activity #1	X		
8	Launch aircraft	Preceded by Activities #1 through #7	X		

we should give some thought as to how activities will be related. For example, one activity may be transporting equipment that will be used by another activity. In such instances, equipment design issues associated with both equipment usability and transportability should be considered simultaneously. It does little good to select equipment in one activity that can't be transported in another activity.

Table 7.1 illustrates an initial work activity categorization for our airplane turnaround example. Based on the information contained in a format like Table 7.1, we can also construct a simple process flow diagram. This flow diagram, however, is created at the work activity level, not the process step level. An activity flow diagram for the jet turnaround process example is illustrated in Figure 7.3. As depicted in Figure 7.3, precursor, successor, and parallel activity relationships occur.

Once these preliminary process characterization steps have been accomplished, we can proceed to the next phase which involves design at the individual activity level. That is, we can begin designing individual activities, such as those identified in Table 7.1. As we begin to work at the activity level, we must always be aware of how the design of an individual activity is affecting the design of the overall

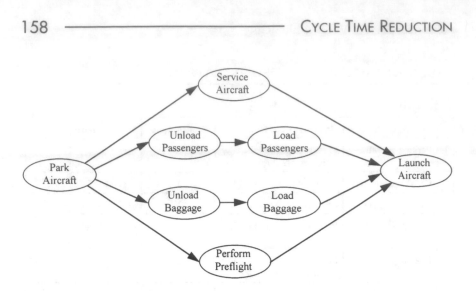

FIGURE 7.3. An activity level process flow diagram depicting the jet "turn-around" process.

process. Therefore, our design efforts must always be iterative, continuously moving back and forth between the process and activity level, as well as among the various activities.

ACTIVITY-BASED WORK DESIGN

The purpose of activity-based work design is to design activities that add as much value to the overall process as possible, especially in terms of optimizing total cycle time. As such, the design process at this level must constantly challenge what value an activity is adding, as well as challenge the value that each of the included process steps are adding. To assist in designing work activities, a general design formula has been created. The formula is called the 7W × 1H Design Formula. It focuses on asking seven questions starting with the letter W, and one question starting with the letter H. As summarized in Table 7.2, the eight questions include the following:

- What activity must be performed?
- Why must the activity be performed?
- What performance parameters must the activity be performed within?

TABLE 7.2. THE 7W × 1H WORK ACTIVITY DESIGN FORMULA

#	Question	Determines
1	What activity must be performed?	Activity purpose, specific activity outputs
2	Why must this activity be performed?	Activity value and output value
3	What performance parameters must this activity be performed within?	Design criteria, needed performance measurements and indicators
4	What environmental conditions must this activity be performed under?	Design criteria
5	What specific process steps are required to complete this activity?	Process flow, cycle time
6	How can each process step be optimally performed?	Selected step method and technology, cycle time
7	What resources are required to successfully perform this activity?	Needed resources, costs
8	When must this activity and all associated process steps be performed?	Schedule

- What environmental conditions must the activity be performed under?

- What specific process steps are required to successfully complete this activity?

- How can each process step be optimally performed?

- What resources are required to successfully perform this activity?

- When must the activity and all associated process steps be performed?

Responses to the questions determine design criteria and other factors. Such other factors include required performance parameters, cost, needed resources, and scheduling. These various factors are summarized in Table 7.2. Remember, when designing at the activity level, always use information created previously in the initial process characterization phase as well.

To better structure the responses to the eight activity-related questions in Table 7.2, a more detailed set of supporting questions and steps have been developed. The design of each activity should follow the following general guidelines:

1. Identify activity purpose and goal.
   • What specifically do you wish to accomplish with this activity?

2. Determine activity value.
   • What specific value does this activity add to the final output?
   • If the activity is eliminated, how will it affect output value?
   • If the activity has low value, should you even proceed with the design? If the answer is no, stop and work on other activities. If yes, proceed.

3. Determine required activity performance parameters.
   • What performance parameters (quality, cost, time) must this activity be accomplished within?
   • What throughput volumes are required?
   • Why are these performance parameters required?
   • Develop a Performance Parameter Matrix, as illustrated in Table 7.3. Use this information as design criteria in steps 5, 6, and 7.
   • Are there any laws, regulations, or standards that specify how this activity must be performed? If yes, then incorporate this information into design criteria. Develop a Regulation Analysis Matrix, as illustrated in Table 7.4. Use developed matrix in steps 5, 6, and 7.

TABLE 7.3. PERFORMANCE PARAMETER MATRIX EXAMPLE

#	Required Performance Parameter	Specific Measurement
1	Quality	1 defect per 10,000 units
2	Total cycle time	1.5 hours
3	Production cost per unit	$13.50 per unit
4	Throughput volume	27 units per hour

TABLE 7.1. REGULATION ANALYSIS MATRIX

#	Regulation, Law, Standard, etc.	Affected Design Criteria
1		
2		
3		

4. **Determine physical conditions (climate, terrain, presence of hazardous sources) that may affect activity performance.**
   - Are physical conditions static or varied?
   - If physical conditions vary, how and when do they vary?
   - How may physical conditions affect activity performance?
   - Will physical conditions affect process flow or required resources?
   - Develop a Condition Analysis Matrix, as illustrated in Table 7.5. Use developed matrix in steps 5, 6, and 7.

5. **Determine required process flow at activity level.** Use all previously generated design criteria input and follow substeps 5a through 5g. Note: Under substeps in Step 5, determine only what must be done. Under Step 6, determine how it can best be done.

5a. Identify all required operation process steps for this activity. Create an initial process flow diagram of only operation steps, as illustrated in Figure 7.4. Also, begin developing a process analysis worksheet for this activity.

TABLE 7.5. CONDITION ANALYSIS MATRIX

#	Possible Encountered Condition	Potential Effects
1		
2		
3		

○   ○   ○   ○

FIGURE 7.4. An initial design of a work activity depicting only operational steps.

- What operation steps are absolutely required to successfully accomplish the work activity purpose and goal?
- Why are these operation steps required?
- How do they specifically add value?
- Can any identified operation steps be combined with one or more other operation steps?
- In what sequence must operation steps occur?
- Can any operation steps occur in parallel?
- Can any operation steps be eliminated if a different process flow design is used?
- If yes, what are the potential tradeoffs in time and cost?

5b. Identify all required transportation steps for this activity. Add transportation steps to the initial process flow diagram, as illustrated in Figure 7.5. Also, add transportation steps as necessary to the process analysis worksheet.
- What transportation steps are absolutely required to successfully accomplish this activity?
- Why are they required?
- Where in the process flow are they required?
- Can any transportation distances be minimized?

5c. Identify all required inspection steps for this activity. Add inspection steps to the initial process flow diagram, as illustrated in Figure 7.6. Also, add inspection steps as necessary to the process analysis worksheet.
- What inspection steps are absolutely required to successfully accomplish this activity?

○ ⇨ ○ ⇨ ○ ⇨ ○ ⇨

FIGURE 7.5. The continuing activity design depicting all required transportation steps.

FIGURE 7.6. The continuing activity design depicting all required inspection steps.

- Why are they required?
- Can any inspection steps be combined with operation steps to create source inspections?
- Can operation steps be made mistake proof so that a needed inspection is eliminated entirely?

5d. Identify all required storage steps for this activity. Add storage steps to the initial process flow diagram, as illustrated in Figure 7.7. Also, add storage steps, if necessary, to the process analysis worksheet.
  - What storage steps are absolutely required to successfully accomplish this activity?
  - Why are they required?
  - If there are intermediate storage steps being designed into the process, why can't such steps be eliminated by transporting goods directly to the next processing or distribution point?

5e. Given the current process flow design for this activity, identify all potential delay points.
  - Why is there a possibility that a delay will occur at a given point in the process flow? Record all potential delay scenarios in the Delay Scenario Matrix, as illustrated in Table 7.6.
  - What can be done to eliminate or minimize all potential delays.
  - Will alternative process flows decrease probability of associated delays? If so, develop multiple "what if" scenarios.

FIGURE 7.7. The continuing activity design depicting all required storage steps.

TABLE 7.6. DELAY SCENARIO MATRIX

#	Delay Scenario	Possible Results
1		
2		
3		

- Include potential delays in the process flow diagram as illustrated in Figure 7.8.

5f. If process conditions should vary, define potential alternative process flow paths.

5g. Continue to develop "what if" scenarios until activity work flow is acceptable and satisfactorily meets all performance parameters and expected physical conditions. Develop multiple iterations and revisions. Save each major iteration for possible subsequent use.

6. **Determine how each process step will actually be accomplished in the most effective and efficient manner possible.** Note: Given different "how to" alternatives selected under Step 6, Steps 5a to 5f may require revision.
   - In developing various alternatives, how can specific technologies assist in increasing process speed at the activity level?
   - What is the specific process function of the technology being considered for use?
   - What are the tradeoffs of using a specific type of technology (e.g., procurement time, cost, equipment reliability and maintainability, capacity limitations, required operator training)?

○ ⇨ ○ ⇨ ○ ▷ □ ⇨ ○ ⇨ ▽

FIGURE 7.8. The continuing activity design depicting all required delay steps. Ideally, no delay steps would be initially built into a process flow diagram.

- How can different transportation modes affect overall process flow at the work activity level?
- How do the different developed "how-to" alternatives affect overall work flow at the activity level?
- Are there any potential conflicts among process steps or work activities as a result of selected methods (e.g., two incompatible technologies)? If yes, resolve.
- Depending on alternatives selected, revise activity process flow diagram developed in Step #5 as necessary.

7. **Based on proposed work flow within an activity and selected means (e.g., technologies) to optimally accomplish each process step, determine all required activity-related resources.**
   - What resources are required for each process step within an activity? Use resource category classification of:
     a. Personnel
     b. Materials and supplies
     c. Tools and equipment
     d. Job-related information
     e. External services
   - To determine required resources, identify:
     a. Resources that have a 100 percent probability of being required.
     b. Resources that have a high probability (but not absolute certainty) of being required.
     c. Low-probability but high-consequence resources.

   Develop a Resource Probability Matrix as illustrated in Table 7.7 and a Required Resource Matrix, as illustrated in Table 7.8.
   - For low-probability, high-consequence resources, develop resource contingency plans, if necessary.
   - To assure immediate resource availability for each process step within an activity, determine resource movement needs. This requires the following information:
     a. What resources (type and quantity) must be moved?
     b. When must they be moved by (time)?
     c. Where must they moved to (destination)?
     d. Where must they be moved from (origin)?
     e. How must they be moved (transportation mode)?

TABLE 7.7. RESOURCE PROBABILITY MATRIX

Resource	Associated Process Step	100% Probability	Very High Probability	Low Probability, High Consequence

      f. What is the most expeditious route between the origin and destination?
- To assure immediate resource accessibility, determine:
  - a. The physical placement and spatial layout of required resources.
  - b. The organization and display of needed resources.
- For required information-related resources, determine who requires what information, when and where. Also determine optimal information retrieval, presentation, and communication means.
- For personnel resources, determine knowledge, skill, and ability requirements. Also determine interpersonal coordination and communication requirements, as well as other team-related issues, if applicable.
- Are any other resources required because of actual or expected environmental conditions under which an activity will be performed? If so, identify and add to resource requirements list.

TABLE 7.8. A REQUIRED RESOURCE MATRIX

Step #	Process Step Description	Personnel	Materials & Supplies	Tools & Equipment	Job-Related Information	External Services
1						
2						
3						

8. **Based on required resources and proposed activity process flow, evaluate for the following:**
   - Any potential delay-generating situations, both at the macro and micro level. If present, how can they be eliminated or significantly minimized?
   - Any major chokepoints.
   - Any conflicts in assuring that the right resources cannot be at the right place and time.

9. **Determine an initial schedule at the activity level.**
   - What process steps must occur when and where?
   - For each process step, what resources are required when and where?
   - Does the process schedule meet cycle time goals as initially defined? If not, reevaluate Steps 1 through 8.

10. **Determine if the activity design meets all other initially identified performance parameters.**
   - If not, reevaluate Steps 1 through 9.

At the end of this second major design segment, you should have a fairly well-designed work activity. This work activity design "package" should include:

- A general characterization of the work activity (e.g., goal, output, performance parameters, environmental conditions, etc.).

- A detailed process flow analysis of the activity.

- Specifics of how each process step will be performed.

- Required resource matrix.

- An initial activity schedule.

Any potential adverse effects at the process level as a result of an activity design should be identified and resolved. The activity-based work design segment should be completed for all identified work activities. In most instances, activities will be designed iteratively and in parallel with each other. For example, a required piece of equipment may be used in more than one work activity. The resultant effect of this requirement needs to be considered for all effected activities simultaneously.

Once all activities have been designed, it is important to assure their proper sequencing and connectiveness. This is accomplished in the final design segment termed *activity integration*.

ACTIVITY INTEGRATION

The final major segment in our new process design effort is termed activity integration. The purpose of this final segment is to assure that all activities are blended into a well-coordinated and integrated whole. This whole represents the total process from beginning to end. As such, work activities, just like process steps, should be seamlessly connected, avoiding unnecessary delays at activity boundaries.

The first step in assuring a continuous and uninterrupted process flow is to construct a final activity flow diagram, as illustrated in Figure 7.9. Then the following questions must be asked:

- How are these activities connected such that no unnecessary delays occur at activity boundaries?

- What integration and coordination mechanisms are in place to prevent process work flow interruptions and resultant delays?

- Who specifically is tasked with assuring the coordination and integration of all associated process-related work activities? Who owns the process that includes the various activities? What are the process owner's specific responsibilities and authorities?

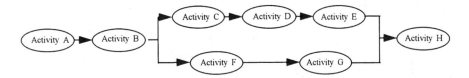

FIGURE 7.9. During the activity integration design phase, it is important to assure that all activities are integrated at the process level.

Once all questions have been satisfactorily addressed, schedules should be fully integrated and finalized at both the step, activity, and process level. Once again, are there any problems or possible delay points? If so, how can they be satisfactorily resolved?

These three major design segments—initial process characterization, activity-based work design, and activity integration—are important general steps in designing any process. Simply thinking about the various questions in each major design segment can add a great deal of value to any process or work activity design initiative. Also, by focusing design attention on what happens in between all of the operation steps, many unnecessary delays can be eliminated or at least significantly minimized. In turn, cycle times can be optimized. Indeed, the overall goal of the design effort should be to better integrate processes, work activities, and process steps, as well as all supporting resources and applicable technologies, so that a fast, coordinated whole results.

At the completion of the three major design segments, an integrated process design package should have been developed. At a minimum, the process design package should include the following:

- A general characterization of the process and all associated work activities (e.g., goals, outputs, performance parameters, expected environmental conditions, etc.).

- A detailed process flow analysis at both the interactivity level and the intra-activity (process step) level.

- Specifics of how each process step and activity will be performed.

- Identification of all required resources.

- A developed mechanism to ensure interactivity coordination and integration.

- An integrated schedule.

The following generic case study illustrates just some of the various factors that must be considered when designing work activities associated with a new or proposed process. In the generic case study, only a partial process design will be described.

CASE STUDY #6

A large, national discount store chain is developing initial plans for a new satellite distribution center to directly supply retail outlets in a major metropolitan area. The proposed distribution center will hopefully allow much faster resupplying of the chain's numerous retail stores, many of which have just recently opened. In addition, the satellite distribution center will resupply outlets in some adjacent communities as well.

A regional distribution center (RDC) owned and operated by the discount store chain, as well as a host of other external suppliers, will transport retail goods to the new satellite distribution center. This continuous supply effort is expected to occur around the clock, seven days a week. Larger, so-called buffer or safety inventories, however, will be stored at the RDC. The purpose of the proposed satellite distribution center is only to receive incoming goods, sort them, and ship them again on outgoing trucks to surrounding retail outlets as quickly as possible. As such, goods are expected to be in the satellite distribution center no longer than 24 hours. Indeed, what is really wanted is a process that provides an almost immediate turnaround of all goods. Ideally, incoming trucks will be unloaded immediately as they enter the distribution center's receiving dock. The unloaded goods will then be instantly sorted and directly transported to a designated shipping dock. Goods will then be quickly loaded onto an outgoing truck and shipped to the correct retail outlet.

The general manager of the discount store chain receives a proposed blueprint and facility layout for the new satellite distribution center. The conceptual building blueprint and facility layout were developed by the company's own in-house engineering staff. With disappointment, the manager feels that the proposed designs are unacceptable in their current state. Furthermore, the initial designs would most likely foster redundant handling of goods, as well as unnecessary intermediate storage steps; conditions that would lengthen cycle times, not shorten them. In addition, the design is actually for a large and expensive warehouse, not a distribution center whose sole purpose is the rapid movement of goods. In fact, the engineering department's proposed design focuses on *storing* goods, not *rapidly moving* goods. Warehouses and rapid distribution centers, suggests the general manager, are not the same thing. Frustrated with the initial design effort, he orders his engineering department to go back to the drawing board and bring him a simple, process flow diagram depicting the distribution center's proposed work activities.

Specifically, the engineering group is instructed to develop a simple, conceptual process model for moving goods rapidly through the distribution center. They are not, however, to design a facility. Once a conceptual process model has been developed, the physical details can then be engineered. The general manager wants the desired process flow model to dictate the facility's design. He does not want the design of the facility to dictate or impose constraints on the desired process flow.

The engineering group uses some applicable parts of the three major design segments of the following:

- Initial process characterization.

- Activity-based work design.

- Activity integration.

Within the first design segment, the engineering group defines the distribution process boundaries as beginning with "initially receiving goods" and ending with "shipping goods to retail outlets." The purpose of the process is to move goods through the distribution center as rapidly as possible. Short cycle times, therefore, are critical. The goal of the process design then is to significantly reduce the redundant handling of goods, as well as eliminate all unnecessary intermediate storage steps. The overall output of the process represents a service that will immediately unload incoming goods, correctly sort them, and rapidly load them on outgoing trucks. Performance parameters include:

- Speed (optimizing the cycle time between receiving and shipping goods).

- Accuracy (assuring that the right goods in the right amount are correctly transported to the right location at the right time).

- Cost (minimizing the additional handling costs per goods received and shipped).

- Breakage (number of goods damaged during handling in the distribution center).

No regulatory or legal constraints are initially identified. Also, besides dealing with a trucking operation, no technological constraints are identified.

The engineering group next defines specific work activities. The three major work activities are initially identified as: scheduling, data management, and goods handling, all of which occur in parallel. As instructed by the general manager, the engineering group will not concern itself with scheduling activities. Instead, it has been instructed to focus only on goods handling, or moving goods from the receiving dock to the shipping dock as quickly as possible. The group also is only to determine what information needs are required for the data management activity. At this stage in the design, the group is not to determine specifically how information will be provided or communicated, nor is the group to determine what specific information technologies are required.

On the basis of these constraints, the engineering group focuses its efforts on the goods handling activity. It is now ready to begin the second activity-based work design segment. It determines that the goods handling activity will consist of unloading incoming trucks, sorting unloaded goods, and loading sorted goods onto outgoing trucks. In the proposed process scenario, full-unit truckloads of goods, both same and mixed, will be received. However, both full-unit loads and individual cases will be shipped on outgoing trucks. The value of the activity lies in the necessity to continuously maintain well-stocked and resupplied retail outlets.

Furthermore, turnaround times for received goods must be no longer than 24 hours, preferably, in near real-time. In addition, the right goods in the right amount must be routed to the right loading dock at the right time without damage or breakage. No adverse environmental conditions should affect the unloading and loading operation.

Once these preliminary design conditions have been considered, an initial process flow diagram is developed. Before beginning, however, additional information is obtained about the scheduling activity. Trucks will be scheduled to arrive and depart so that, in many instances, goods can be immediately unloaded in receiving and directly transferred to shipping. Yet, due to such variabilities as weather, traffic, scheduling conflicts, and partial loads, some delays will occur between receiving and shipping. In such instances, the intermediate storage of goods will be required. On the basis of this information, three process scenario flow paths are developed. The designed flow paths incorporate the concept of crossdocking. Crossdocking refers to moving goods directly from receiving to shipping in a distribution center without prolonged intermediate storage. Three categories of goods movement are identified as the following:

- Current/Active—The direct transfer of goods from receiving to shipping.

- Current/Short Term Storage (Current/STS)—goods requiring a short, intermediate storage period (less than 2 hours) before direct transfer to shipping.

- Future/Longer-term Storage (Future/LTS)—goods requiring a longer intermediate storage period (up to 24 hours).

These three postulated flow paths are graphically illustrated in Figure 7.10.

On the basis of the three process scenarios, the following general operation steps are initially identified as the following:

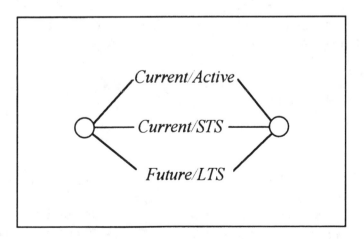

FIGURE 7.10. Three postulated flow paths for the goods-handling activity.

- Unloading, which refers to the initial unloading of a truck at the receiving dock.

- Sorting of individual cases and unit loads, which will determine the immediate destination point of the goods (e.g., directly transporting goods to a waiting truck in shipping or to an intermediate storage site).

- Loading, which refers to loading outgoing trucks at the various shipping docks.

- Storage unloading, which refers to the unloading of goods and placement into an intermediate storage site.

- Storage reloading, which refers to the loading of goods at an intermediate storage site for transport to a waiting truck in shipping.

Further review and evaluation of these operation steps indicate that initial unloading and sorting can be combined into one operation step—unloading/sorting. These combined operational steps are possible if material handlers know the immediate destination of each unit load or individual case. This requires two types of information— what specific goods are on each truck, and the immediate destination of those goods (e.g., to go directly to a waiting truck in shipping or to an immediate storage site).

In addition, storage unloading and reloading actually represent rework because the goods are being handled more than once. In this case, however, scheduling dictates this necessity, and the two steps are left as operation steps. At the end of this review, four general operation steps remain.

1. Unloading/Sorting.

2. Loading.

3. Storage unloading.

4. Storage loading.

These four operation steps with accompanying step designator numbers, are placed along the three flow paths, as illustrated in Figure

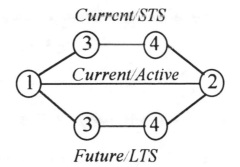

Current/STS

Current/Active

Future/LTS

FIGURE 7.11. An initial activity design depicting only required operation steps.

7.11. Note that all three flow paths begin with operational step 1, Unloading/Sorting.

Next, required transportation steps are identified. Three possible transportation steps are determined as the following:

- Transportation from unloading/sorting to loading (from receiving to shipping).

- Transportation from unloading/sorting to an intermediate storage area.

- Transportation from storage loading at an intermediate storage area to loading (e.g., from an intermediate storage site to a waiting truck in shipping).

These transportation steps are placed along the three proposed flow paths with the previously identified operation steps. This revised flow diagram is illustrated in Figure 7.12. The engineering group also notes that in the final facility layout, transportation distances must be minimized in order to shorten process cycle times.

Inspection steps are considered next. It is decided that the inspection of goods for breakage and damage can occur at the same time that the goods are being loaded and unloaded by the material handlers. Therefore, no separate inspection steps are built into the system. Rather, they are combined with the four operation steps, as illustrated in Figure 7.13.

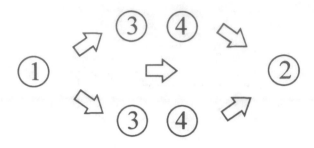

FIGURE 7.12. An initial activity design depicting added required transportation steps.

Required storage steps are identified next. As noted previously, storage will be required with two of the three flow paths— Current/STS and Future/LTS. These storage steps are illustrated in Figure 7.14. The difference between the two bottom flow paths in Figure 7.14 is the duration of the intermediate storage period— short-term (less than 2 hours) versus long-term (greater than 2 hours but less than 24 hours).

On the basis of Figure 7.14, potential delay scenarios are developed next. It is decided that most delays can be avoided if, and this is a big if, accurate information is continuously received on what goods will arrive when, and what is their immediate destination (e.g., to shipping or intermediate storage). This information must also be

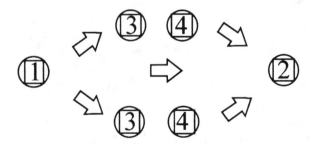

FIGURE 7.13. An initial activity design depicting added required inspection steps. Note that inspection steps have been combined with operation steps to form source inspections.

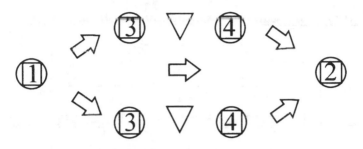

FIGURE 7.14. Final activity design depicting added required storage steps.

made available to material handlers at the time they are handling goods in the various receiving, storage, and shipping areas.

The proposed goods-handling activity developed by the engineering department would work something like this: in the Current/Active flow path, goods are unloaded in receiving and directly transported to a waiting truck in shipping, where they are immediately loaded and shipped. No intermediate storage steps are required in this first flow path. The goal of the proposed activity design is to have the Current/Active flow path used approximately 60 percent of the time. In the Current/STS flow path, goods are placed in a staging area or possibly on a conveyor system for release later that day (e.g., within 2 hours). It is predicted that this flow path will be used 30 percent of the time.

Finally, the Future/LTS flow path consists of transporting goods to a different staging area from the Active/STS staging area. There, goods would be temporarily stored until final shipment. Shipment in the Future/LTS path would occur later than two hours after storage, but less than 24 hours. This least efficient flow path, it is hoped, will only be required 10 percent of the time.

Along with the proposed process flow diagram, the engineers also create a generic overhead view diagram of the various suggested flow paths. This bird's-eye process perspective is illustrated in Figure 7.14. Engineering also makes some suggestions concerning related equipment selection. These suggestions include using an automatic truck-loading dock mechanization, as well as a wireless and remote electronic data interchange system.

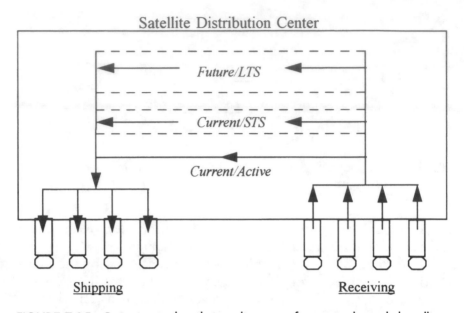

FIGURE 7.15. Generic overhead view diagram of proposed goods-handling flow paths.

They next briefly consider the third phase of the design process, activity integration. It's obvious that the efficiency of the goods-handling activity is dependent on the scheduling and data management activities. To make the proposed process work, near real-time information will be required. Without having immediate access to information concerning what goods go where and when, numerous delays will quickly creep into the designed process. The engineers realize that they have designed a process dependent on the rapid distribution of accurate and timely information. This is based on a workable and usable computer-based information system.

The engineering group presents the high-level process design to the general manager. They realize that through good process design and information management, a large and expensive warehouse-type facility isn't required after all. It is estimated that with the proposed process model, goods will need intermediate storage only 40 percent of the time, not the 100 percent that was used in the initial facility layout.

The general manager is quite pleased with the approach the engineers have taken. He instructs them to provide a detailed "how-to" analysis, complete with all technical specs, required resources, and estimated costs. He further instructs them to provide a more detailed, micro-level analysis of required process steps within the goods-handling activity.

SUMMARY

Just as an existing process can be redesigned to increase process speed by eliminating unnecessary and time-consuming delays, so can a new process be designed to prevent such delays from occurring in the first place. In designing a new process, however, it is important to actually focus design efforts on the process, and not only on the operation. As noted, operational design does not equate with process design.

Process design can be divided into the following three major design segments:

- Initial process characterization.

- Activity-based work design.

- Activity integration.

Under activity-based work design, the following questions must be considered:

- What activity must be performed?

- Why must the activity be performed?

- What performance parameters must the activity be performed under?

- What environmental conditions must the activity be performed under?

- What specific process steps are required to successfully complete the work activity?

- How can each process step be optimally performed?

- What resources are required to successfully perform this activity?

- When must the activity and all associated process steps be performed?

At the end of the three design segments, an integrated process design package is available for use. The process design package should include the following:

- A general characterization of the process and all associated work activities (e.g., goals, outputs, performance parameters, expected environmental conditions).

- A detailed process flow analysis at both the interactivity level and the intra-activity(process step) level.

- Specifics of how each process step and activity will be performed.

- Identification of all required resources.

- A developed mechanism to ensure interactivity coordination and integration.

- An integrated schedule.

It is always important to remember that work activity integration and coordination are necessary in design efforts if optimal process speed is to be ensured.

# 8 ———————— SUMMARY

In the previous chapters, a number of basic principles essential to achieving the competitive dimension of speed have been explored and described. For many businesses and industries today, the ability to decrease cycle time as represented by the amount of time required to move from one defined point in a process to another is becoming the determining factor between profit and loss. In today's and tomorrow's business environments, economies of speed are rapidly replacing economies of scale.

As noted by futurists Alvin and Heidi Toffler, authors of the much publicized book *Creating a New Civilization,* in post-industrial, information-intensive Third Wave economies, the speed of operations and transactions will greatly accelerate.[1] As a result, businesses will be pushed closer and closer to operating in real time. Time wars will replace price wars. This new speed reality will certainly tax existing corporate infrastructures, technologies, and management skills. It will also necessitate organizational change at an almost unprecedented scale. Indeed, the ability to transform slow, high-cost, cumbersome, industrial-style bureaucracies into lean, fast, flexible organizations, is perhaps one of the greatest challenges facing the corporate world today. Unfortunately, many corporations still fail to recognize this reality cascading down upon them. One can only hope that such blind ignorance will not cause irreparable damage that can only hasten an unsuspecting corporation's ultimate demise.

This required quest for speed should not be viewed, however, as applying only to the private business sector. The need for speed is relevant to any organization, irrespective of specific affiliation or even nationality. The United States Army for example, is beginning to realize that its future success will greatly depend on its ability to rapidly mobilize and deploy troops to threatening hot spots, many of which will occur in remote, inaccessible locations. Well-equipped forces that can enter a spreading conflict quickly will have a significant advantage over slower, less equipped foes. Joint Chiefs of Staff Chairman John Shalikashivili captures this strategic advantage best when he observed that, ". . . the sooner forces arrive at the scene of a conflict, the fewer you need." According to Shalikashivili, rapid logistics and transportation processes with supporting airlift capability may be more decisive in winning a future battle than a fleet of high-tech stealth bombers.[2] Shalikashivili is not the first military leader to recognize the importance of speed in battle. That honor perhaps goes to the Chinese military strategist Sun Tzu, who wrote more than 2,000 years ago that "speed is the essence of war.[3]"

As the competitive and strategic importance of speed is increasingly realized, it is hoped that organizations can apply many of the ideas and techniques presented in *Cycle Time Reduction* that are directly applicable to any work setting, irrespective of business, industry, or government affiliation. A short review may help summarize some of the key points made in each chapter.

Chapter 1 identified many of the benefits associated with reducing cycle time. Some of these benefits included the following:

- Increased productivity.
- Better utilization of available human and nonhuman resources.
- Greater responsiveness to meeting customer needs.
- Decreased costs.
- Greater use and return on assets.
- Greater ability to rapidly exploit narrow windows of opportunity.
- Increased schedule reliability.
- Faster growth rates.
- Improved profitability.

Chapter 2 described how the quest for speed must begin with the elimination of time-consuming process waste, represented by unnecessary and non-value-adding process steps and activities. Such steps and activities only add delay and additional cost to any work process. By systematically analyzing and mapping processes and associated work activities, non-value-adding steps can be identified and then either eliminated, minimized, or combined with a value-adding step.

A key point made in Chapter 2 is that speed flows from simplicity, especially simple work processes devoid of non-value-adding process steps that cause unnecessary delays. Another important point made is that the time devil is almost always found lurking in the details. That is why it is so important to fully understand a work process at the micro, detailed level. Unfortunately, for many companies, such detailed process understanding is completely lacking or only fragmentary at best. In such companies, erroneous process perceptions replace accurate process realities.

As noted in Chapter 2, a detailed process understanding is especially critical for companies involved in high frequency, short turnaround types of service or manufacturing activities. Small time savings in such activities can quickly accumulate into major annual savings. Such major time savings, in turn, can represent significant cost savings and substantial increases in productivity.

Chapter 3 explored the necessity for having the right resources at the right place and time. Frequently, process delays are caused by waiting on a needed resource. Such resource-related delays can be caused by not having resources available when and where they are required. They can also be caused by not having resources immediately accessible and reachable. Issues associated with resource availability generally involve how to get the right resource to the right place at the right time. Issues relating to resource accessibility involve how to best place, organize, and display tool, equipment, and information resources within an immediate work setting.

As noted in Chapter 3, any associated single delay caused by resources not being immediately available is usually much longer than a single delay associated with a resource not being immediately accessible. However, resource accessibility-related delays, represented by numerous mini transportation-delay-transportation retrieval sequences, can quickly accumulate into significant total delay times. It is always important, therefore, to focus cycle time reduction efforts on eliminating or at least minimizing delays associated with both resource availability and accessibility.

Chapter 4 discussed how technology, especially computer-based information and communications technologies, can be a useful ally in reducing cycle time. Technology, despite its frequent advertisement to the contrary, does not represent a magical panacea for all of our cycle time-related inefficiencies. Technology is basically neutral. It's how we use it that counts. Without considerable process fore-thought, most technology applications result in expensive failures. However, with initial process understanding and planning, technology can reduce process cycle times in a number of valuable ways. Some of these include the following:

- Eliminating various steps from a process.

- Minimizing the time duration of associated process steps.

- Combining two or more process steps.

- Improving resource availability.

- Improving resource accessibility.

In Chapter 5, the concept of continuous flow was introduced. Continuous work flow refers to the continuous flow of products, materials, information, goods, people, and just about everything else. In continuous work flow, everything moves continuously, stopping only when value is directly being added. Process steps and activities in continuous work flow become interdependent elements of a larger, single process, seamlessly connected.

To achieve the ideal of continuous flow and associated theoretical cycle time outlined in Chapter 5, all unnecessary delays and other non-value-adding steps must be identified and eliminated. All required resources also must be made immediately available and accessible at the right time and place. Continuous flow is frequently impeded by the presence of a few significant delays that represent major process chokepoints. Only a few such delays can account for a disproportionate amount of the total cycle time of any process. Sometimes process chokepoints are caused by work volumes exceeding the capacity limitations of available machine and human resources. At other times, periodic work surges may strain existing resource capacities, thereby temporarily interrupting process flow. Work leveling can sometimes help moderate such surges. The physical layout of a work process also can cause numerous interruptions and delays in work flow. By better aligning the physical layout to mimic process flow or higher frequency flow paths, significant improvements in continuous work flow and associated reductions in cycle time can be achieved.

Typically, work processes and activities cut across organizational boundaries, both at the division, department, and intradepartmental levels. Chapter 6 discussed this cross-cutting relationship of processes and noted some of the resultant negative effects on cycle time. In most instances, cross-functional cooperation, coordination, and communication are required to accomplish work in an efficient and rapid manner. Unfortunately, organizational "stovepiping," company politics, turf battles, inefficient communication channels, and differing departmental priorities and agendas preclude or significantly decrease such required cooperation and coordination. These organizational realities prevent effective functional handoffs, resulting in process delays being created at divisional and departmental boundaries. Getting divisions and departments to focus on company processes and priorities in a coordinated and cooperative manner is perhaps one of the most difficult challenges faced in reducing cycle time.

In some instances, the creation of multidisciplined, cross-functional work teams focused on completing a specific work activity can help reduce the need for such close intraorganizational cooperation. Members of cross-functional work teams are normally drawn from throughout an organization on an as needed basis, irrespective of division or department affiliation. It is important to note that the use of cross-functional work teams represents a very significant change in organizational configuration. Not solely because it is a team-based approach as frequently thought, but because it is a work-based approach. That is, instead of configuring people around traditional functions and disciplines, cross-functional work teams represent an attempt to organize people around work itself. In essence, small, self-contained, organizational modules with all of the right resources are created to complete a specific work activity or group of related activities.

Chapters 2 through 6 focused on reducing the cycle time of an existing process. In Chapter 7, that focus switched to the initial design of a new process or work activity. The emphasis was placed on preventing non-value-adding process steps from being built into a process in the first place. A major objective of Chapter 7 was to concentrate the design effort on the process itself and not the operation, as is commonly the case. As noted, an operational design does not equate with a process design. In process design, all associated steps (e.g., transportation, inspection, storage, delay) and activities are considered in a systematic and integrated fashion. Process design can be divided into the following three major design segments:

- Initial process characterization, which focuses on gathering basic information at the process level.

- Activity-based work design, which focuses on designing individual work activities and all associated process steps, as well as identifying all required resources.

- Activity integration, which focuses on assuring the optimal integration of all individual activities so that a cohesive and well-coordinated process whole forms.

These three major segments are normally performed in an iterative, circular fashion, continuously moving back and forth among the process, activity, and process step levels.

The outcome of a process design initiative is a comprehensive process design package, that includes the following:

- A general characterization of the process and all associated work activities (e.g., goals, outputs, performance parameters, expected environmental conditions, etc.).

- A detailed process flow analysis at both the interactivity level and the intra-activity (process step) level.

- Specifics of how each process step and activity will be performed.

- Identification of all required resources.

- A developed mechanism to ensure interactivity coordination and integration.

- An integrated schedule.

As noted in Chapter 7, whether reducing the cycle time of an existing process or designing a new process, the basic principles repeatedly discussed and illustrated in *Cycle Time Reduction* are still applicable. These basic principles involve the following:

- Eliminating process waste.

- Providing the right resources at the right place and time
- Using technology, especially computer-based information technology, to improve process flow.
- Creating continuous work flow.
- Using cross-functional work teams focused on completing a specific work activity.

As suggested, these five basic principles are relevant to any work environment, irrespective of business, industrial, or government affiliation. Indeed, these five basic principles seem almost universal in any cycle time reduction initiative. To better capture the myriad of factors, both large and small, that can potentially affect cycle time, a summary checklist has been created. The summary checklist, captured in table format, is illustrated in Table 8.1.

TABLE 8.1 A SUMMARY OF FACTORS NEGATIVELY AFFECTING CYCLE TIME

	Some Factors Negatively Affecting Cycle Time
1.	Unnecessary and non-value-adding work activities.
2.	Linear process flow as opposed to the use of parallel process flow.
3.	Redundant, time-consuming, and/or unnecessary transportation, storage, delay, or inspection steps.
4.	All rework steps.
5.	Recurring sequences of delay - transportation - delay steps situated between operation or inspection steps.
6.	Intermediate storage steps and associated redundant handling of materials.
7.	Inefficient or redundant transportation routings.
8.	Redundant material packaging, unpackaging, and repackaging.
9.	Inspections not combined with an operation step whenever possible.
10.	Needed resources that are not immediately available at the right time and place.
11.	Needed resources that have not been previously identified for a process step.

TABLE 8.1 *continued*

12.	Poor resource accessibility that causes recurring transportation - delay - transportation resource retrieval sequences between operation steps.
13.	Inefficient use of technology that unnecessarily lengthens cycle time.
14.	Process layouts that do not mimic process flow or the highest frequency flow paths.
15.	Process layouts that cause extended transportation distances and times.
16.	Major chokepoints (megadelays) that constrict process throughput and flow.
17.	Work volume that continuously or temporarily exceeds throughput capacity.
18.	Delays at interdepartmental or interdivisional boundaries.
19.	Organizational structures that impede continuous work flow.

Having read and studied *Cycle Time Reduction*, you will still undoubtedly have some unanswered or unresolved questions. That's good, since we're all still learning how to best achieve this new dimension of speed—this next step in the continuous improvement journey. However, you may have generated one especially nagging and puzzling question regarding cycle time. That is, just exactly how fast is fast enough? The answer to this frequently asked question is surprisingly simple. Fast enough is *always* just a fraction faster than the competition!

GLOSSARY

7W × 1H design formula   a design formula for designing individual work activities. The formula centers around seven questions that begin with the letter w and one question beginning with the letter h.

Activity   a logical grouping of several process steps. Various related work activities comprise a process.

Activity-based work design   a process design method that focuses its efforts at the work activity level and the integration of those activities.

Actual capacity   refers to the realistic or expected capacity of a human or machine resource. Actual capacity equals theoretical capacity multiplied by resource availability.

Autonomation   refers to machines equipped with attached sensors so that the machines stop automatically whenever a problem occurs.

Before-after chart   a chart that compares the before-and-after cycle times and costs of a proposed process improvement or redesign.

Capacity   potential output of a human or machine over some allotted time period.

Chokepoint   a major delay that accounts for a disproportionate amount of cycle time.

Combination step   a process step that combines two or more process steps, such as an inspection and operation step.

Contingent resources   resources that have varying probabilities of being used in a process, but not a certainty of being used.

Continuous flow refers to products, materials, information, goods, people, and just about everything else, moving continuously, stopping only when value is directly being added. In an idealized continuous flow, there are no delays and process cycle time equals theoretical cycle time.

Continuous improvement normally refers to the incremental improvement of a process. However, improvements normally fall along a continuum, from small to very large.

Continuous work activity a work activity that is ongoing.

Convergent flow a process containing two or more parallel and separate flow paths that merge into a single linear flow path.

Critical path cycle time in a process containing more than one flow path, the amount of time required to progress through the longest flow path from beginning to end.

Crossdocking moving goods directly from receiving to shipping without prolonged, intermediate storage.

Cross-functional work team a small group of individuals representing multidisciplines who are dedicated to completing a specific work activity. Team members usually come from multiple divisions and departments.

Cycle time the amount of time required to move from one defined point in a process to another.

Data summary chart a chart that summarizes basic process-related information such as number of steps within each step category, all cumulative associated step times, and process-related cost data.

Decision branch a branching point in a process that entails making a decision to select the next appropriate flow path.

Delay step an unscheduled delay of materials, parts, information, goods, or objects. Delays also include any human waiting time.

Divergent flow   a process that splits into two or more separate and parallel flow paths.

Electronic performance support system   also referred to as EPSS. A computer-based tool designed to provide job-specific information such as procedures, schematics, reference information, expert advice, etc. on demand.

Hypothetical capacity   the theoretical or ideal potential output of a human or machine over some allotted time period.

Inputs   the initial ingredients of a process. Inputs include people, materials, equipment, information, procedures, capital, and policies.

Inspection step   includes quality and quantity inspections, reviews, and authorizations.

Intermittent work activity   a work activity that is only performed on a periodic basis. Periodicity may occur on a set or random schedule.

Linear flow   a process flow that contains only sequential steps, one after another.

Mobile technologies   normally refers to computer-based and communication technologies that can be easily carried and operated in a stand-alone fashion without requiring an external power source or some other external source (e.g., telephone line). Examples include notebook computers, cellular telephones, and personal digital assistants.

Operation step   any value-adding step that directly moves a process forward. Normally represents a human or machine action step.

Operations design   a design which focuses only on required operational steps and does not consider other related process steps.

Outputs   what is transformed from a specific set of inputs. Process outputs normally include producing some type of product or offering some type of service.

Parallel process   two or more separate process flows occurring simultaneously.

Personal digital assistant   also called a PDA, represents a small, hand-held, portable computer that also has communications capabilities such as data transfer and faxing. Represents a mobile technology.

Process   the transformation and blending of a set of inputs into a more valuable set of outputs.

Process analysis   a systematic analysis that collects all quantitative process-related data, including time, costs, required resources, and process flow. Identifies both value-adding and non-value-adding process steps and activities.

Process analysis worksheet   a specific format used in collecting process-related data, including step description, process flow, required time, needed resources, etc.

Process design   the design of a complete process, as opposed to only designing required operation steps.

Process flow   the sequencing of either process steps or activities which depict various types of flow paths (e.g., convergent, parallel, divergent) and various precursor and predecessor relationships.

Process flow diagram   a symbolic representation of a process. Symbols can either represent individual process steps or work activities.

Process layout   the physical design of a process area, including the location of required workstations, machines, equipment, and supplies.

Process overhead-view diagram   a bird's-eye sketch of a process. A process map graphically depicting the location of various process steps, the sequence of steps, and the various flow paths.

Process product analysis a process analysis that focuses on what is being done to an object in a process.

Process reengineering refers to the radical redesign of a process. Commonly contrasted with continuous incremental improvements.

Process task analysis a process analysis that focuses on a human or machine action. What a human or a machine is doing to an object.

Process waste all non-value-adding process steps and activities. Waste only adds time-consuming delays and unnecessary process costs.

Resources represent various process inputs. Resources are frequently grouped under personnel, materials and supplies, tools and equipment, job related information, and external services.

Resource accessibility describes the relative ease with which resources can be immediately identified and retrieved within an immediate work area.

Resource availability refers to the degree to which resources are ready for use.

Resource contingency planning a set of plans that deals specifically with acquiring contingent resources in the most expedient manner possible.

Rework any unnecessary, repeated operational step.

Risk equals probability of an event happening multiplied by the consequences associated with that event happening.

Seven-Step PI Method a systematic method of analyzing a process and reducing all associated cycle times.

Source inspections immediately performing an inspection at the site of an operation. A source inspection combines an operation and transportation step.

Step   a fundamental unit of any process or work activity. There are six basic process-related steps: operation, transportation, delay, inspection, storage, and rework.

Storage   any scheduled delay of materials, parts, goods, semi-finished or finished products.

Theoretical cycle time   an ideal cycle time. The amount of time consumed by only value-adding steps and activities in a process.

Total cycle time   the amount of time required to progress from the beginning to the end of an entire process. Compare with cycle time, which may refer to only a specific portion of a process and not the complete process.

Transportation   any action that moves something. Transportation steps include moving objects, goods, information, and people.

Value-added/non-value-added chart   a pie chart depicting the ratio of value added step times or costs to non-value added step times or costs.

Virtual work activity   a work activity that occurs only once in a process and is not repeated.

Wireless   an expression that refers to mobile technologies that can transmit information without being physically connected to some communication medium such as a telephone line.

NOTES

1 The Need For Speed

1. George Stalk, Jr., "Rules of Response," *Perspective* series, The Boston Consulting Group, Inc. 1987. Also see George Stalk, Jr. and Thomas M. Hout, *Competing Against Time* (New York: The Free Press, 1990).
2. E. Yost, *Frank and Lillian Gilbreth: Partners for Life* (New Jersey: Rutgers University Press, 1949).

2 Process Waste

1. Jerry Harbour, *The Process Reengineering Workbook* (New York: Quality Resources, 1994).

4 Speed and Technology

1. E. L. Cochran, "Control room user interface technology in the year 2000: Evolution or revolution?" *Proceedings of the Human Factors Society 36th Annual Meeting*, 1992, pp. 460–464.
2. Louis S. Richman, "Managing Through A Downturn," *Fortune*, August 7, 1995, pp. 59–64.
3. William Scott, "Atlas Expands 747 Fleet, Serves Niche Cargo Market," *Aviation Week & Space Technology*, December 5, 1994, pp. 35 & 38.
4. Harry Peterson, "Logistics, Transportation and Distribution: Engineering Service and Profits," *Industrial Engineering*, December, 1993, pp. 21–24.
5. George and Emily Stevens, *Designing Electronic Performance Support Tools— Improving Workplace Performance with Hypertext, Hypermedia and Multimedia* (New Jersey: Educational Technology Publications, 1995).
6. Tim Dowding, "Emerging Technology: Interactive Maintenance Support Systems," *Performance & Instruction Journal*, April, 1994, pp. 7–9.

6 Cross-Functional Work Teams

1. Louis S. Richman, "Managing Through A Downturn," *Fortune*, August 7, 1995, pp. 59–64.
2. William Bridges, *JobShift* (New York: Addison-Wesley, 1995).

8 Summary

1. Alvin and Heidi Toffler, *Creating A New Civilization—The Politics of the Third Wave* (Atlanta: Turner Publishing, Inc., 1994).
2. Quote taken from *Aviation & Space Technology*, March 6, 1995, p. 17.
3. Samuel B. Griffith, *Sun Tzu The Art of War* (London: Oxford University Press, 1963, p. 134).

ABOUT THE AUTHOR

Jerry L. Harbour is the manager of Industrial Engineering for the engineering and contracting firm of Mason & Hanger-Silas Mason Co., Inc. Author of *The Process Reengineering Workbook*, Harbour has extensive experience in a variety of domestic and international industrial settings. He holds a Ph.D. in Applied Behavioral Studies from Oklahoma State University and a B.A. and M.S. in Geology.

INDEX